Her Candle Burns at Both Ends

ANN COSTELLO

iUniverse, Inc.
New York Bloomington

Her Candle Burns at Both Ends

iUniverse books may be ordered through booksellers or by contacting:

iUniverse
1663 Liberty Drive
Bloomington, IN 47403
www.iuniverse.com
1-800-Authors (1-800-288-4677)

ISBN: 978-1-4502-5510-3 (pbk)
ISBN: 978-1-4502-5511-0 (cloth)
ISBN: 978-1-4502-5512-7 (ebk)

Library of Congress Control Number: 2010912977

Printed in the United States of America

iUniverse rev. date: 9/20/2010

For Deirdre

Contents

Author's Preface

I was always confident that my children would remain reasonably healthy. They would never succumb to any life-threatening illness—after all, I believed, I could never survive anything like that, so therefore it would not happen.

For many years, I had worked as an ICU nurse, caring for people who were critically ill. Always mindful and empathetic about their mental and physical well-being, I had a healthy objectivity that was necessary to deliver essential supports for healing.

In April of 2008, my twenty-five-year-old daughter, Deirdre, had been teaching in Japan for a year. When she called me one night to say that she had been diagnosed with acute leukemia, a life-threatening disease, I went into total denial.

After spending almost twenty-four hours a day in Deirdre's hospital room, I came to know firsthand the emotional, spiritual, and physical turmoil that patients and families go through. I was eventually faced with a vital decision and a responsibility concerning her treatment. My previous "meant to be" and "going with my intuition" philosophies were put to the ultimate test.

Over a year after I received the phone call on that April night, Deirdre inspired me to write and relay the story of our ordeal, of the unconventional counselling that has helped me immensely, and of the many different elements of love that enabled us to triumph over despair and sadness.

Acknowledgments

I am thankful to my editor, *Patricia Thomas*.

Thank you to the people who have given me the confidence to create this book:

To *Deirdre,* for inspiring me to write.

To *Joan Hall Hovey,* mystery novelist, for her notes of encouragement as I began to write.

To Deirdre's emissaries, *Deborah Young* and *Kelliena,* who told me to keep writing.

I am indebted to numerous people:

To my children, *Aisling, Deirdre,* and *Conor,* for being who you are.

To our friends and relatives, who gave immeasurable support during the most trying time of our lives.

To the nurses, doctors, and staff at the VG Hospital in Halifax, who took such special care of Deirdre during her illness.

Introduction

My daughter, Deirdre, has always been very persuasive. She knows what she wants and goes after it. Whether it's a Dairy Queen sundae, an expensive dress, a trip, a working stint in Japan, or having someone write a book about her, she gently finds a way to accomplish her goals.

In 2008, after she was diagnosed with acute leukemia, she and I went to battle together to fight the disease. Deirdre took up arms of hope, strength, and resolve; I took up arms of hope and faith.

In the summer of 2009, she slowly persuaded and inspired me to write about our experiences throughout her leukemia treatment: the chemotherapy, the invasive investigations, our joyful and sorrowful moments, our hope that never wavered.

Our story starts when Deirdre is living in Japan and the diagnosis is suddenly made. It continues with her time in the hospital in Halifax and the challenges of adjusting to life when she is discharged home. We want to share the story of how we coped with terrifying events and how our love transcended any dejection I might have felt. Deirdre displays her incredible insight, courage, and strength as she deals with the adversities that assail her during the illness. Throughout it all her quirky sense of humour remains intact.

As the story ends, Deirdre conveys her message of love in unique ways.

I would like to share the story of how our love allowed my mind to open up to experiences I never dreamed were possible.

Chapter 1

SHOCK AND DENIAL

Take life for what it is. Try to be a good person (not blind) and love every minute of it. Take from it all that I can. Always be open to new things, places, and *experiences.*—Deirdre's diary, 2001

It is early March 2008.

Deirdre Porter is twenty-five years old. She looks forward to a future filled with love and happiness. She has taught English in Japan for nearly a year now and has grown to love the country and its people. She and Daichi recently met and fell in love. Three weeks ago, they spent a wonderful weekend snowboarding in northern Japan. She is about to embark on a career in graphic design. Life has never been better.

Aisling Porter, Deirdre's sister, is twenty-eight years old. She is in second-year medical school at Dalhousie University in Halifax and lives in her own apartment downtown. When her sister and best friend, Deirdre, left for Japan last March, she cried for days. Since then she's gotten over it, happy that Deirdre is content with her life in Japan. Aisling is working toward a career that suits her to perfection, and she can look forward to a bright future. She has a special group of friends close, loyal, and positive. Life has never been better.

Conor Porter, Deirdre's brother, is twenty-two years old. He is taking time off after spending a few years in college. He is independent, lives in his own apartment, and is finding his own way in life. Life has never been better.

And I, Ann Costello, their mother, have a nicely balanced life. I do casual nursing assignments in various Nunavut communities, and while at home in Halifax, I work as a casual nurse in the post-anaesthetic care unit at the local

1

hospital. I like to travel, dance, ski, and read, and I look forward to whatever other interesting activities I might find. I live alone in a nice little house not far from downtown.

My children have learned to fly on their own and know that I'm always here for them. They are healthy and compassionate as they continue to grow through new life experiences. Last summer, all four of us travelled around Japan for two weeks, an experience filled with delightful and unforgettable memories. Life has never been better.

A few days ago, while we chatted on the phone, Deirdre mentioned that she had a sore throat, generalized achiness, and nausea. I was a little concerned but was reassured when she told me that the weekend before, she had seen a doctor in the emergency department of the local hospital. He had diagnosed strep throat. Penicillin is the drug of choice for strep, but Deirdre has a penicillin allergy. He prescribed a four-day course of Zithromax, a strong and usually very effective antibiotic. He also mentioned something about having blood tests if she didn't improve, but he said her family doctor would recommend them if needed.

I hoped for a one-month assignment in Nunavut, starting in the next few weeks. On two separate occasions, after arrangements were finalized, obstacles got in the way and prevented it from happening. I've learned that obstacles crop up for reasons we don't always understand, and that some things are just not meant to be.

Deirdre called again around mid-March; she felt as badly as she had the last time we talked, even though she'd completed the course of antibiotics. Despite taking regular painkillers, her joints ached most of the time. She saw her family doctor, who told her she still had the flu. She continued to work, but was forced to take more days off, too weak and sore to leave her bed.

"One day I even started crying at work because I was so sick," she wrote in one e-mail.

By March 31, every joint and muscle ached, and it had become increasingly difficult for her to move. At intervals she felt feverish, nauseated, and short of breath.

After another unsatisfactory visit to the same doctor, she called me and explained her symptoms. I thought she might have rheumatic fever, a disease precipitated by strep throat. The doctor, Deirdre said, still hadn't taken her basic vital signs or given her a physical exam.

I pleaded with her to come home. Told her I would book her ticket. She was confident that she just had the flu—like the doctor told her.

On Thursday, April 3, Deirdre called with an update. She was losing weight; her appetite had decreased considerably. She had seen the doctor again that day; he still hadn't checked her vital signs or done a physical exam.

Deirdre said that after he noticed her enlarged lymph nodes around her neck—lumps she'd noticed weeks earlier—he gave her a requisition for blood tests and told her to go to a nearby clinic at 9:00 AM the following morning. He knew that within the past six months, except for visiting Tokyo, northern Japan was the only place Deirdre had been. It was winter in Tokyo, yet he assumed she had contracted a disease from a bug bite. Aware of her signs and symptoms over the past four weeks, and aware of her emaciated state, he still advised her to go to work; she dragged herself home to bed.

Over the phone, I pleaded with her to let me book her flight home. It was becoming more and more evident that she urgently needed proper medical help.

"You will be too sick to travel in a few more days, Deirdre," I said.

"I'll wait and have the blood tests done," she answered. "I'll call you right away with the results. I'm sure it won't be anything much."

After I put the phone down, I meditated and prayed that it wouldn't be anything serious, that my fear was just that of an overly concerned mother. I sat at my computer by the kitchen and checked the flights from Tokyo to Toronto. There were seats available on the weekend, but Thursday and Friday were fully booked. The alternative was Tokyo to Vancouver to Halifax.

Could Deirdre make that long journey? Could she last until Saturday? My mind was racing like it was on a treadmill.

Thursday night came. I called Deirdre's cell phone twelve times between 10:00 PM and 1:00 AM, and 10:00 AM and 1:00 PM (Tokyo time). When there was no answer, I assumed her phone battery had died. She should have the blood results by now.

As I lay in bed I pondered the serious illnesses she could have. Was she really bitten by a bug as the doctor suspected? The suggestion seemed ludicrous. *Is he crazy?* Bugs don't live in cold weather. In Tokyo last summer I didn't see any, but then again…

I desperately tried to convince myself that I was overreacting, hoping to dispel the tentacles of panic that tried to grip at my insides as I lay in the dark. *If Deirdre does have a disease caused by a bug bite, surely there is an antidote or treatment available?*

What was wrong with me? When Aisling and Deirdre backpacked through various parts of the world for months at a time, I never worried about them. I was confident in their ability to take care of themselves, confident their spirits would guide them. I began to meditate, and I prayed that everything would turn out well in the end. At 1:00 AM, exhausted, I finally drifted into a facsimile of sleep.

At 2:00 AM the phone on my bedside table rang. It was Deirdre. The battery on her phone had died; she was using Daichi's cell. My heart was already pounding and my fingers began to sweat as I waited to hear about the test results. I made an intense effort to sound calm and composed when I asked her about them.

There was silence on the line for about ten seconds.

"I have leukemia," she cried, her voice quivering. "They've just given me a blood and platelet transfusion. I'm on antibiotics and steroids and I have to leave right away if I want to get treated at home. They don't want me to travel, but I told them I had to get home."

My mouth and tongue had dried to a crisp during that fifteen-second revelation. Though I felt numb all over, I attempted to reassure her, making great efforts to hide my broken, hoarse voice.

"I'm sure it's not leukemia, Deirdre," I said. "After all, they've been wrong in the past few weeks. You probably have lupus, which is very treatable. Your blood is abnormal because you are so run-down. I'll book your flight and you can leave right away." It was 2:00 PM Friday (Tokyo time). The flight to Toronto was leaving at 5:00 PM.

Lupus, though it has signs and symptoms that are similar to leukemia, is not nearly as life threatening. In acute leukemia (cancer of the blood) the bone marrow produces malignant white blood cells that cause damage and death by destroying vital red cells, normal white cells, and platelets, and by spreading to other organs in the body. At Deirdre's young age it runs rampant, hence the urgency for treatment.

"I feel a bit better now," she said. "I'd rather wait until tomorrow so I can rest tonight. I'm so tired. I just want to sleep."

After I agreed to wait a day and said I'd book the flight and e-mail her the itinerary, I continued my spiel of reassurances with as much optimism and pretence as I could muster. I was in a haze of confusion and could not envision the extent of her illness. I would call her that evening.

Unable to talk for long, she ended the conversation, saying that Daichi would look after her and take her to the airport.

After I put the phone down, my whole body began to shake uncontrollably. I had surpassed the tears, the hand-sweating, and the heart-pounding stage. My teeth were chattering as if I were out in -20°C weather without a coat.

Deep breathing didn't work. I was beyond praying, and couldn't concentrate enough to book Deirdre's flight. I didn't know what to do. I was unable to talk, so I couldn't call anyone. My precious daughter, Deirdre, was ill and on the other side of the planet, in a foreign country where she couldn't speak the language. She would have to make that long journey home alone, in her fragile state.

Could I meet her in Tokyo?

There wasn't enough time. In this, the most terrifying and horrific time of her life, I was powerless to rescue my child, whom I adored.

Ten minutes later, with no letup on the shaking, I reached into the cupboard for a glass and poured a vodka and ginger ale. After three drinks, I slipped into mild oblivion and the shaking stopped. I rarely drink hard liquor, but whatever worked to calm me was quite acceptable then.

My hands settled down, allowing me to push the appropriate computer keys one at a time. I learned the 5:00 PM flight was totally full. Mercifully, Saturday's flight was only half full, and there were three empty seats available for her to lie across. I was slightly under the influence, but finally able to concentrate and focus. I settled myself in front of the computer to book Deirdre's flight home.

When I clicked on the "wheelchair assistance" icon, a message came up. Air Canada needed seventy-two hours' advance notice, and medical approval, if any passenger had one of a number of medical conditions; leukemia was one. Despite the soothing effects of the vodka, my legs weakened at the thought.

Deirdre could not wait that long. I clicked the icon to minimize that window and opened my e-mail. I would encourage Deirdre to make it through security on her own. She would have Daichi to help her get that far. She could let the flight attendant know her predicament when they were airborne. With prayer and Deirdre's determination, it was doable. I switched back, completed the booking, and e-mailed the information to her. The flight would arrive in Halifax at 11:00 PM on Saturday, April 5.

Conor, Aisling, and Deirdre—September 1990

It was 6:00 AM when I finally grasped two hours of sleep. Before that, I meditated and prayed to my spirit, to my deceased mother, and to whatever spirit guide could help Deirdre on her journey home. I was in shock and denial as I paced around the house. I still couldn't talk. I had to analyze and unravel this bizarre turn of destiny. Alone.

Finally, I rationalized that she definitely did not have leukemia; it was all a mistake so I wasn't going to bother Aisling or Conor with this news. I would let them know on Saturday afternoon, April 5, before Deirdre's flight landed at 11:00 PM.

In total denial, I decided I would go about my normal day.

Chapter 2

Journey Home from Japan

Faith consists in believing when it is beyond the
power of reason to believe.—Voltaire

On Friday morning, April 4, Aisling and I were to meet for coffee. I knew if I faced her, it would be impossible to hide the nightmare that was happening so I called her and cancelled our date. I kept the telephone conversation to a minimum, explaining my plans for the day. She had an important exam to write and then a class that afternoon.

The facade worked. She remained blissfully ignorant and would be spared the agonizing thirty-hour wait until Deirdre's arrival.

At 8:00 AM, when I opened my e-mail, there was a message from Deirdre.

"Got the itinerary. Feeling better after all the meds and stuff."

Throughout the day I busied myself with everyday domestic chores. Occasionally, when a bout of anxiety assailed me, I took a few minutes to pray to my spirit, asking for Deirdre's safe return home. The interlude of prayer enabled me to continue with the mindless chores.

By 7:00 PM (7:00 AM the next day in Tokyo) I couldn't wait any longer to call Deirdre. She picked up the phone on the first ring. Her voice sounded stronger. She said that, unable to sleep, she and Daichi had been awake most of the night. They talked and made plans for him to visit her in Halifax. He had important exams coming up the following week. After that, he would come.

"I feel a lot better," she said. "The medicine and stuff have made me feel better than I have in days. I'm just so scared right now about the long flight." Hearing these words made my stomach turn. I wanted to do the

7

impossible—go to Tokyo and accompany her home—but all I could do was offer words of encouragement.

"I'll be praying for you, Deirdre," I said. "I saw on the Air Canada Web site that there are lots of empty seats on that plane. Tell the flight attendant about the leukemia after you are airborne. I'm sure they'll do what they can to make you comfortable."

"Okay, I'll do that," she answered.

The transfusions had given her body more fuel to work with, for now. The steroids temporarily masked the symptoms of pain and discomfort.

I told her I'd call her around 4:00 AM (4:00 PM Tokyo time). She would be at the airport by then, waiting for her flight to leave. We said our good-byes.

That time spent talking with Deirdre pulled me out of denial and pushed me into the reality of what was really happening. After I put the phone down, I felt a surge of overwhelming anxiety, like I was being pulled into a dark hole.

A minute later, I was jolted by the ring of the phone. It was my friend, Mollie, on the line.

"How are you?" she asked.

"Oh, fine," I said, trying to sound calm.

We'd talked for less than a minute when she asked about Deirdre. She knew Deirdre hadn't been well in the past few weeks. There was a lull on the line as I decided how best to answer this question.

"Deirdre might have leukemia," I said. "She's coming home tomorrow and she'll need chemotherapy treatment right away."

"I'm coming over right now." She hung up.

I felt relieved to finally put the nightmare of the last eighteen hours into words.

Mollie, who lived two streets away from me, was at my doorstep in less than five minutes. We sat on the green leather couch in the living room, and between my sobs, I recounted my living nightmare. After I finished telling her everything and calmed down, she gently suggested that I must let Aisling and Conor know.

"I'll wait until nearer to the time of her arrival," I said, still intent on sparing them the agony of knowing their sister was so sick and then having to wait the long hours for her arrival.

"I think you should call Aisling now," Mollie said in a kind but firm tone.

"I think you're right," I said. "I'll call her right now."

Aisling and her friends were out celebrating after writing their big exam that day. I called her cell phone but she didn't answer so I left a message asking her to call me. When she called back I missed it—didn't even hear the phone ring. She called again half an hour later. Despite the fact she'd had a few glasses of wine, she later told me she sensed something was wrong, because normally I would leave a message with my reason for calling. She knew that Deirdre had been sick and asked if she was okay.

"She's coming home tomorrow," I said in a broken voice. "They think she might have something like leukemia, but I'm almost certain it's not that. I'm sure they don't have the right diagnosis."

"I'm coming up to your house now," she said. "Somebody will give me a ride." She hung up.

I called Conor but he wasn't home.

Mollie and I met Aisling at the front door. We embraced, and tears flowed down our cheeks. A few minutes later, we sat on the couch and I told her everything. She had studied about leukemia in medical school and was aware of its life-threatening magnitude. She wanted to speak to Deirdre right away. She picked up the phone and punched in the number; she said hello to Deirdre almost immediately.

"What have you been doing, girl?" she asked in a cool tone, temporarily pushing away any signs of her anxiety. While Aisling walked up and down the stairs to her bedroom, a drink in her hand, Mollie and I chuckled and listened to her loud bravado.

"You should milk the most out of this, Deirdre," she said. "People will feel sorry for you, so they'll be running around waiting on you hand and foot. I'll get you fluffy magazines and junk food and you can just lie in bed and enjoy all the attention."

Twenty minutes later, when she finished the call, our tears of sadness had turned to tears of laughter.

Mollie left at 10 PM.

Aisling and I, in a numbed state, sat and made a list of what to buy for Deirdre's hospital stay. We wanted to do something concrete while we waited for her return, and on some level we knew that to do something might push aside the sporadic stabs of worry and make time pass more quickly. The thought of Deirdre, alone on this tedious journey, made me shudder.

Aisling stayed that night.

Unable to sleep, I lay awake worrying and tried to think of other illnesses Deirdre could have. I tried to decipher why this was all happening and what I could possibly do to change the situation. With no answers, I prayed to every celestial being to guide her safely home.

Finally, 4:00 AM came and I could call Deirdre again. When I dialled her number, she answered after two rings. She had just gone through security in Tokyo airport and was waiting to board her flight. Thank God she had made it that far—one less obstacle to overcome. She sounded more upbeat than earlier, perhaps trying to hide how miserable she really felt. I had no idea of the gravity of her illness.

Daichi had looked after her until then. She said he was heartbroken that he couldn't accompany her, but with exams coming up it just wasn't feasible. He would see her in Halifax in a couple of weeks.

"He was crying and more upset than I was," she said later. "But I felt all right, knowing that he'd visit me."

I could only imagine his pain as he watched her go through the security gate.

In the hour after that, I had sporadic thoughts of the flight being cancelled or that she would have to wait hours and hours at the airport. I worried she would have to go back and end up in a hospital in Tokyo.

But I also knew that with Deirdre's strength of resolve to get home, she would get on that plane despite her weakened state. I was further relieved one hour later when I read the status of her flight on the computer—it had just left Tokyo Airport.

The next day, Aisling and I went shopping for Deirdre between hourly visits home to check the flight status. We kept ourselves busy all day long. I cooked one of Deirdre's favourite dishes: beef stew with parsnips, potatoes, carrots, and onions, all in a leek soup base. Later in the afternoon, Conor came by the house and I told him about Deirdre. Unaware of the gravity of leukemia, he didn't worry and I didn't enlighten him. He would learn more in the next few days.

Late in the afternoon, I spoke to a nurse who had worked with leukemia patients. She convinced me that Deirdre did have leukemia. After speaking with her, I was still optimistic that she would recover. I was also aware of the long road ahead. I was prepared to spend the rest of my life taking care of her—I just wanted her to live.

At 6:00 PM the phone rang. It was Deirdre. She had made it to Toronto; she was in Canada. She had slept through most of the journey thanks to the kind flight attendant. Deirdre said that once the plane was airborne, she could no longer pretend that everything was okay and she had started to cry. After she explained her illness, the flight attendant took Deirdre to the back of the plane where there were three empty seats. Deirdre lay across them and the flight attendant covered her with blankets.

Succumbing to exhaustion, she slept for most of the journey. The steroids had done their job in keeping pain and discomfort away. I was impressed with the medical team's prudent foresight. Their plan of treatment was allowing her to make it home in reasonable comfort.

While we talked on the phone, she ended the conversation abruptly, too weak to stand by the payphone any longer. She was waiting to be assisted onto the Halifax flight that was leaving in one hour.

Aisling and I were elated and wrapped our arms around one another. In a few hours we would be holding Deirdre. What an extraordinary sense of relief.

Chapter 3
THE HOMECOMING

Smooth seas do not make skilful sailors. —African proverb

The flight from Toronto was due to arrive on time, at 11:00 PM. We were at the airport at 10:00.

We stood a few feet away from the sliding glass doors and watched some of the last passengers trickle out. As we continued our vigilant watch for Deirdre, our eyes were glued to the hall she would come through.

At last, there she was—sitting in a wheelchair, her shoulders drooping, her eyes sunk back in her head. Her hair was highlighted a golden yellow, stylishly cut at the base of her neck. She wore a trendy light green coat and burgundy boots.

Overjoyed, and with uncontrolled eagerness, I walked through the doors. A stern security guard, sitting at a desk inside, ordered me back. When Deirdre was wheeled through the doors, I knelt beside the wheelchair, wrapped my arms around her, and held her tightly for a few minutes without saying anything.

"I love you so much, Deirdre," I said after I found my voice. "I'm so happy you're home at last. I know you're going to recover from all this." Despite her frail and weak appearance, her face lit up with a radiant smile. Aisling and Conor, delighted to see her, stepped forward and hugged her in turn.

Up close I saw that her neck lymph nodes protruded visibly. Her complexion was grey and unhealthy looking. An eczema rash that had been widespread over her body for the last five years was no longer there. She looked like she weighed about one hundred pounds—forty less than when I saw her the previous summer. My fears were allayed by my utter delight to have her home safely. I looked at her debilitated state and believed that with appropriate medical treatment in Halifax, she would be back to herself in no time.

Overwhelmed and exhausted from the journey, she had few words at first. I knelt beside the wheelchair, holding her hand while we waited for Aisling and Conor to bring the car up to the door.

Too weak to handle more, she had brought only a purse and a small, half-filled knapsack. I knew how fragile her immune system was and I was anxious to leave the crowded terminal. As soon as Aisling drove up to the door, I helped Deirdre walk to the car and we left for home.

During the thirty-minute car ride, she talked about the plane journey from Toronto. Sitting upright on the narrow plane seat had been tortuous. Throughout the two-hour flight, her head ached and she felt nauseated and weak.

"I don't know what I would have done if it had been like that all the way from Tokyo," she said, letting out a sigh of relief. Later that night, I thanked the spirits who had guided her safely to Halifax.

When we arrived home, she looked excited to be back—she walked around the house checking out everything.

"It's so good to be home," she said with a smile on her face.

I was shocked when I watched her walk around. She dragged her feet slowly and methodically like an old woman—presenting a contrast to the highly energetic young woman she had been just months before. Until I saw her, I did not appreciate how ill she was.

How could she have worked in this state? How could a doctor have seen a patient this ill and ignored her symptoms? Why hadn't I been more persuasive, brought her home sooner? I wasn't aware of her abnormally high pain threshold this time, to her detriment. She had tolerated the extreme pain so well that those close to her failed to notice the extent of her illness.

After walking around for less than five minutes, Deirdre lay down on the green sofa in the living room. I put two pillows under her head and draped a blanket over her. The room has a ten-foot-high ceiling, an old gas fireplace, and a hardwood floor. Books, Inuit carvings, and photographs line two sets of bookshelves and the fireplace mantle.

Deirdre had lived in the house for extended periods of time while I was in Nunavut; she liked to sit and read in this room. She had a flair for interior design and I rarely purchased furniture or any kind of decor without her approval.

While Aisling and Conor chatted with Deirdre, I went to the kitchen and filled four bowls with the hot stew. Deirdre's face lit up when I set them on the glass coffee table.

"I've been looking forward to this." She took a spoonful of stew and held it under her nose. "Oh, that smells so good," she said.

We sat and ate together. Deirdre ate a small portion and looked like she enjoyed every little bit of it.

After she finished, she laid her bowl on the coffee table and picked up her knapsack from where it was propped up against the couch.

"I've got something for you guys," she said, a big grin on her face. "I really wanted to bring you home something from Japan." She handed us each a key chain with a Japanese emblem on the end of it. She said that before she left for the airport in Tokyo, she went to a little store near where she lived to get these for us.

We knew very little about Daichi—Deirdre was happy to fill us in. One day, that previous January, she was in a bank near where she lived, trying to explain to the teller about the loss of her bank card. She needed a replacement but was having no luck communicating this. Daichi stood behind her and noticed their difficulty in communicating. He offered to translate.

"He was actually blushing when he came up and offered," she said, smiling. Daichi had lived in California for three years and was fluent in English. After everything was sorted out, they talked for a while and Daichi invited Deirdre for coffee. That was the beginning of their relationship.

She went on to tell us that two weeks before she came home, Daichi had asked her and his parents to dinner at his apartment. It was the first time Deirdre had met his mother, and the language barrier made communication difficult. Midway through the dinner, Deirdre suddenly felt very weak. Embarrassed, she excused herself from the table and lay down on a couch. Daichi explained Deirdre's persistent flu to his mother.

Deirdre had met his father a month before and had a delightful time with him. He was fluent in English.

She told us about the nightmare trip to the clinic—that while she and Daichi made the fifteen-minute walk to the train station, she was forced to stop frequently. She was short of breath, dizzy, and in constant pain all over her body. The train was crammed full with no seating room. On Japanese trains, there are designated seats for elders and the physically handicapped, but it's not necessary to offer one's seat to a sick or weak-looking person—not in the rules.

To avoid falling down, she sat on the floor.

When she arrived at the clinic, the nurses immediately took her vital signs. They were all abnormal. She had a fever of 40°C. She was transferred onto a stretcher and given boluses of intravenous (IV) fluids, pain medication, and antibiotics. Because she had her periods and had a low platelet count, the doctor worried about a hemorrhage. Platelets maintain the balance between bleeding and clotting. The normal range is two hundred to three hundred; Deirdre's platelet count was nine.

After the doctor read the blood reports, he took Daichi aside. Deirdre, unable to speak or understand Japanese, watched them talk. Already sensing some terrifying news, she waited, dreading what he would tell her. Later she said, "I knew it was something really bad when I saw the look on the doctor's and Daichi's faces while they talked." Daichi was left to break the news of the nightmare.

She said that he cried nonstop as he explained about the leukemia. She felt numb. With Daichi as an interpreter, the doctor explained that chemotherapy treatment would kill the cancer cells that caused the leukemia, and that she would recover. She took solace from this news, and told the doctor she wanted to come back to Canada for treatment. He reluctantly agreed, and told her that she needed transfusions and other medications before she could make the trip; she must leave immediately after that.

After she received blood and platelet transfusions and an IV antibiotic, the doctor prescribed a course of steroids, hoping to forestall pain and discomfort during the journey home.

She said that after they got home from the clinic, Daichi cooked a dish called *nabe*. *Nabe* is a traditional Japanese dish made with vegetables, tofu, fish, and other healthy ingredients. He had futilely cooked healthy meals for her in the previous few weeks, hoping to reverse the insidious deterioration of her health. Even so, she became too weak to do simple housework such as washing dishes or doing laundry. Showering took great effort.

She was glad to be home, though it was obvious she missed Daichi already.

Before going to bed, she called Daichi. When she began to talk to him, I could tell by the enchanted look on her face that this was something more than just a passing relationship.

We went to bed around 1:00 AM. I decided to wait and take her to the hospital in the morning. It was a five-minute drive from my house.

I was awake, worrying, when Deirdre tiptoed into my room at 2:00 AM.

"I'm getting a bad headache," she whispered, almost apologetically.

"Maybe we should go down to the emergency department?" I asked.

"That's probably a good idea," she answered.

I turned on the light and put together a bag for Deirdre with a nightgown, housecoat, slippers, toothbrush, and toothpaste. After we got dressed we made our way down to the emergency department (ER).

When we got to the triage area, a young paramedic dressed in navy blue scrubs took her vital signs. I explained the gravity of her condition to him. Her blood pressure was critically low, heart rate high, with no fever—the steroids had taken care of that.

I was quite concerned about her weakened immune status and her propensity to catch some bug. It was Saturday night, a few drunk people were shouting and swearing, and the place reeked of alcohol. After I told one of the nurses about my concerns, she immediately led us into an isolation room. A doctor came and examined her.

The headache and low blood pressure were a result of dehydration. After the nurse took blood samples, she inserted an IV in Deirdre's arm and gave her a litre of fluid through it. This temporarily raised the blood pressure to a normal level. The headache subsided after she had the fluid and painkillers and by then she felt much better.

While the IV fluid was going through, Deirdre lay on her side on the stretcher, dozing off and on. I sat in a chair beside her and chatted quietly with some of the nurses who came and went. We had worked together in an ICU a number of years ago. One nurse recalled how animated I used to be when I told stories about Deirdre; Deirdre was a child then.

She recounted one story of when Deirdre went to a dance competition and bought a whoopee cushion at one of the souvenir stalls; at that time Deirdre's interest lay more with the stalls than the competition. When she brought the whoopee cushion home, she took great delight in hiding it and embarrassing her victims with the farting sound it produced when they sat on it. Deirdre, who was half-awake on the stretcher, smiled when she heard some of the stories.

The doctor in Japan had given Deirdre an envelope to bring to the medical staff in Halifax. It had her blood results and other reports in it. After the ER doctor read and photocopied them, he gave them back to us. I was astounded when I read the results: White blood count (WBC): 97,000 (normal range 4,000 to 10,000), platelet count: 9 (normal range 150 to 350), red cell count: 6 (normal range 12). The high WBC indicated the leukemic cells had multiplied substantially. The low platelet count put her in danger of hemorrhaging, and the depleted red cells that carry oxygen around the body could have compromised her breathing. The leukemic cells were killing healthy cells, like weeds that kill flowers or vegetables.

The blood test results from the emergency department that night showed very little change from the earlier tests. The transfusions that were given in Japan had been a temporary solution. Only chemotherapy would reverse the disease.

The hematologists—the leukemia specialists—would not be in the hospital until 9:00 AM and Deirdre would have no further treatment until they had seen her. It was now only 5:00 AM, and the isolation room didn't have a bathroom. Deirdre had to use the same one as the other patients, which by now was filthy. I suggested that we go home until the hematologists came in. The staff agreed.

After we arrived home, we slept for a short period before the phone rang.

Daichi and Deirdre—April 3, 2008

Chapter 4

ADMISSION TO HOSPITAL

I like living. I have sometimes been wildly, despairingly, acutely miserable, racked with sorrow, but through it all I still know quite certainly that just to be alive is a grand thing.—Agatha Christie

The ringing phone woke me. When I answered it a nurse from the hospital asked for Deirdre. Her tone had a sense of urgency. I told her that Deirdre was sleeping but that I could take a message.

"She needs to come to the emergency department right away," she said. "The hematology resident is here. She has seen Deirdre's reports and she needs to be admitted this morning."

"I'll bring her in now," I said, and put the phone down.

Aisling and Deirdre were already awake and came into my room. Deirdre said she felt better. After I told them what the nurse said, Aisling insisted on driving Deirdre to the hospital.

Exhausted, I agreed. I went downstairs and put the kettle on while they got ready. I made tea and toast, which they had before leaving. As they headed out the door, I asked them to call if they needed me. I would make my way down to the hospital in a few hours. Ten minutes later, I was back in bed and fell asleep right away.

At 11:30, a few seconds after I woke up, I felt a heavy weight lodge in my stomach as my life flashed before me. What would become of Deirdre? *I should be with her right now.* I sat up in bed and prayed and pleaded to my spirit and to whatever deity could help us get through this ordeal. After a few minutes, I called the emergency department and was told that Deirdre had been transferred to the Victoria General Hospital (VG), a twenty-minute walk from my house.

After I put the phone down, I quickly showered and fumbled around in the closet for clothes. I pulled on a pair of jeans, a green turtleneck sweater, socks, and black, low-cut boots. I ran downstairs, grabbed my short brown coat, gloves, purse, and a yellow umbrella. I ran most of the way to the hospital, jaywalking when the road was clear, barely aware of the sound of the raindrops that hit my umbrella.

When I arrived in the lobby of the hospital, Mollie was waiting for me. It was comforting to see her. After we hugged, I unloaded my anxieties, telling her about the night before as we walked along and stepped into the elevator to go to the eighth floor.

We arrived on 8B and found our way to a little kitchen outside the side entrance to the unit. It had a table covered with a yellow and red vinyl tablecloth and it sat under a window that faced out onto other hospital buildings. A fridge stood against a wall next to the table. It was stocked with several bottles of water for patients' use, cans of club soda, and food brought in by families. A bulletin board hung on a wall on the other side. It had inspirational notes and poems pinned to it; reading them made an interesting distraction. Pictures of former patients hung on the walls.

Tea and coffee were available for patients and families.

Mollie walked with me as far as Deirdre's room and then left to go home. When I opened the door and saw Deirdre, my heart plummeted to my stomach. She sat on top of the bed, fully dressed, rocking back and forth, her face contorted in pain and fear. She was vigorously kneading her left thigh with both hands, as if it were torturing her. Aisling and Conor looked confused and petrified as they took turns massaging her left arm, desperately trying to ease the pain that seared through her muscles and nerves. I ran and sat beside Deirdre and put my arms around her.

Eyes wide with fear and apprehension, she looked straight at me. She said the pain was so bad she thought she was going to die.

"But I can handle the pain, as long as I can live," she cried.

"Of course you'll live, Deirdre," I said, struggling to reassure her. Inside I was swamped with apprehension. "I'll explain to the nurses how bad the pain is. Maybe they'll give you a morphine drip that will get rid of the pain." The nurses were giving her intermittent doses of IV morphine but those didn't touch this unrelenting pain.

I went out to the main desk opposite Deirdre's room and explained the intensity of the pain to the nurses. One of them came into the room immediately. When she saw Deirdre's state, she injected another dose of morphine through the IV and then went outside to get the necessary equipment for a morphine drip. We continued to massage Deirdre's arm and thigh—she said doing so helped ease the pain a little.

A few minutes later, the nurse returned and moved quickly to set up the drip. She hung the bag with the morphine on the IV pole, threaded the IV tubing through a cassette in the pump, and pressed a few buttons, which started the flow of the liquid. She continued to inject intermittent doses of morphine every five minutes until the drip took effect.

Ten minutes later, at maximum dose level, the morphine drip dulled the pain. The atmosphere in the room relaxed as Deirdre's eyes slowly closed, and her head and shoulders settled back into the pillows. Looking across at me, Conor and Aisling exhaled deeply, shaking their heads.

Conor went to the cafeteria and brought us each a slice of pizza with salami, cheese, and green pepper. After he ate his in the kitchen, he came to stay with Deirdre while Aisling and I went out and had some.

Aisling told me about the scenario in the emergency department that morning. After Deirdre was settled onto a stretcher, a female resident did a complete medical history and physical exam. The resident explained the urgent need for chemotherapy treatment that would arrest the significant progression of the disease.

Treatment would begin on Wednesday, following numerous investigations. Strict isolation precautions were necessary. The resident went on to say that she would start Deirdre on an IV antibiotic, discontinue the steroids, and give more IV fluid. Ten minutes before her transfer to the VG hospital, Deirdre began to experience severe pain in her left arm and left thigh. She was given two Tylenol 3 pills.

"It was horrendous," Aisling said, putting her hand over her forehead and shaking her head. "The move from one stretcher to another and the ambulance ride made her pain worse. The pain pills were useless. Conor and I came in the ambulance with her.

"The pain was driving her crazy. She was crying while we helped her massage her arm and thigh all the way here. Conor and I felt so helpless. I'll never forget it as long as I live."

The pain was caused by the leukemic cells that crowded the bone marrow, affecting the surrounding nerves and muscles; it is sometimes called "bone pain."

Because of the accumulation of leukemic cells, her liver and spleen were swollen. Her skin was speckled with numerous petechiae (pinpoint red dots under the surface of the skin caused by bleeding), a result of the low platelet count. Chemotherapy would kill the leukemic cells but also the good cells. The good cells would rejuvenate after the effects of the chemo drugs wore off.

The bone marrow transplant unit on 8B had the strictest isolation precautions in the hematology department. It was rare to admit a patient with newly diagnosed leukemia to this unit, but the delay in treating Deirdre's illness rendered her much more debilitated than was usual on admission.

Back in the room, Deirdre woke up after sleeping for an hour. Her face was drawn and tired looking. After she was awake for a while, she sat upright in the bed and looked around the room.

"I feel better," she said. "I feel a bit high, but it's better than that awful pain. I like it here. I'm glad I have my own room and I don't have to go anywhere else. I'll be glad to have the chemo over with."

The room was about nine feet by fourteen feet. To the left of Deirdre's bed was a big window that looked onto the parking lot and other hospital buildings. The room had its own bathroom just inside the door. It also had a TV, a telephone, and wireless Internet. The room had a small sink, cupboards, and two paper towel dispensers hanging on the wall to the right of the bed. A bulletin board and a whiteboard hung on the wall facing the bed. By the window was a large armchair that could extend to a lying position. There were two small visitors' chairs. The unit had been renovated in recent years.

Coats, shoes, and purses were not allowed in the unit. There were locker rooms for them, off the corridor outside. The main entrance to the unit—at the north end of the corridor—had two large doors with glass panels. Only large equipment, such as beds, stretchers, and wheelchairs, was allowed through these doors. A large red laminated sign, taped to the doors read, "Entry Strictly Forbidden."

Visitors and staff entered through a small anteroom on the side. It had a large sink for hand washing. A green container of alcohol liquid, Manorapid, used for hand cleaning, hung on the wall above the sink. Before entering the unit, everybody was required to wash their hands with soap and water and clean them again with the undiluted Manorapid.

The unit had six rooms. A metal cart with gowns, gloves, and masks sat outside each room. Before entering the rooms, hands had to be cleaned again with the Manorapid that hung outside the doorway. Masks and gowns had to be worn while visiting post-transplant patients; this was not a requirement in Deirdre's case.

Later that first afternoon, Deirdre was taken by wheelchair to the third floor for a chest X-ray. I walked alongside, pushing the IV pump, while the porter rolled the wheelchair along. He talked a lot, and I could sense Deirdre's irritation as she rested her head on her hand, looking pale and weak. We waited outside the X-ray room for about ten minutes before she was taken into the room. As soon as the X-ray was done and she emerged from the room, I wheeled her back to the unit.

She said her head was aching. After she returned to her room the nurse gave her two codeine pills. I put a cold facecloth over her forehead. She slept for a little while and when she woke up the pain had gone.

Chapter 5

INVESTIGATIONS

Too often we underestimate the power of a touch, a smile, a kind word,
a listening ear, an honest compliment, or the smallest act of caring,
all of which have the potential to turn a life around. —Leo Buscaglia

I thought it would enhance Deirdre's recovery if one of us stayed in her room every night. I wanted to watch over her like I had when she was a few hours old. I stayed during the week and Aisling stayed on the weekend. The staff was supportive of whatever would bolster Deirdre emotionally and physically. They provided a cot for us, which I put by the wall facing the foot of the bed.

Some mornings, Deirdre and I laughed as I struggled to uncurl my spine from the crooked mattress. One night, I woke up and sensed her looking down at me.

"What's wrong?" I asked.

"You look so small and quiet under those covers. I wondered if you were alive," she said, sitting upright and craning her neck like a giraffe.

The following day, preparations for chemotherapy continued. Swabs were taken and more blood was drawn for testing. After her blood was grouped and cross-matched, she received another unit of blood and platelets. Despite their busy day, the nurses explained every treatment and procedure in detail, with ease and confidence. They encouraged us to express any concerns we had. Their profound dedication to this type of nursing was evident as they provided comfort to us all during this trying time.

They quickly grew very fond of Deirdre. Regardless of how wretched she felt, she showed them respect, politeness, and charm.

She was weak and vulnerable from this brutal whirlwind of change and became extremely dependent on me. I knew she hated asking for help but often I could sense her needs. She found it easier to refuse when she didn't need something than to ask if she did. Until all of this, she had been remarkably independent.

When she was fifteen, she and Aisling ran an Irish dance school in Halifax and taught every Saturday. During her summer breaks from university, she worked in Ireland and Yellowknife and roamed around different parts of Europe. Confident about her own astute decision-making ability, she took wise, calculated risks as she continued to grow and move forward gracefully— dancing with the flow of life.

On Monday, the array of investigations began. Although the morphine drip kept her reasonably comfortable, she still required occasional doses of codeine. She had a belly-button ring that needed to be removed. It had been there for about seven years and she had tried unsuccessfully to remove it herself. She was afraid to let anybody touch it. Four nurses, Aisling, and I all failed in our attempts to take it out. It was stuck there like a barnacle on the bottom of a boat.

We used a ring cutter and forceps, to no avail. Finally, Aisling manoeuvred the clasp with her fingers and slipped it out. Deirdre had her hands over her face for most of the half-hour procedure.

"*Phew!* I'm glad that's gone," she sighed after it came out. "The morphine helped a lot."

At 11:00 AM, the staff hematologist, Dr. White, came into the room and introduced himself. He was soft-spoken, pleasant, and in his late thirties. He explained the plan of care and asked Deirdre if she had any questions. She had none.

In preparation for the MRI, Deirdre wore a hospital gown. Metal and electronic objects that would interfere with the magnetic field in the MRI room were forbidden.

Donna Boyd, the nurse looking after Deirdre that day, disconnected the IV lines and IV pump. She gave Deirdre a sedative, Ativan, to help her relax during the procedure. A porter came and took her by stretcher and I walked along beside her.

"I'm a little scared," she said as we went down in the elevator.

"You won't feel a thing," I assured her. I explained to her about lying on the narrow table in the cylindrical tube—that the table would move back and forth during the imaging, and that she would hear thumping noises from the machine. I told her I would be standing behind a glass divider not far away.

"Take deep breaths when you're in the cylinder. Imagine you're scuba diving, and the top of the cylinder is the ocean above you."

"That's stretching it," she laughed. I told her a story of when I accompanied a patient to the MRI room a few years back. While I helped the patient onto the table, scissors sprung from my pocket, got sucked into the cylinder, flew across to the other side, and stuck to the roof.

After we got to the room, the technicians helped Deirdre onto the narrow MRI table. They put coils (little wires) around her head. Before she was pushed into the cylinder, I squeezed her soft, smooth hand and then went behind the glass window. Twenty minutes later, when the stretcher emerged from the cylinder, she looked more relaxed than I expected.

"I thought about Daichi and me snowboarding," she said. "That and the Ativan helped me relax."

Shortly after getting back in her room, Dr. Nebojsa Sparavalo, with his thick eastern European accent, came by to do a bone marrow biopsy. Even though the blood tests gave a lot of information on the leukemia, the biopsy would give an in-depth evaluation of the type of leukemia, the numbers of cells, and other details. When he explained the procedure to Deirdre, she didn't understand a word, but nodded her head and smiled. The nurses and I had already told her about it. A few minutes later Aisling arrived.

The resident, a nurse, and a lab technician walked into the room. The lab technician wheeled a metal trolley in front of her. It carried glass tubes, specimen bottles, glass slides, and other laboratory supplies.

Deirdre wore a pale green hospital gown for the procedure. She lay in bed on her left side in a fetal position. Aisling and I sat on chairs facing her. Her witty sense of humour remained intact. I had mentioned her fear of the biopsy to the staff. Standing to the right of her, preparing the needle for freezing, Nebojsa asked why she was scared and asked what she knew about a bone marrow biopsy.

"I saw something about it in a movie," she said.

"What angle did they show it from?" he asked.

She replied to his question by extending her arm out and pointing to her face, implying that the actor's face had a tortured expression. "This one," she said. Gales of laughter filled the room.

"I like this sense of humour," Nebojsa roared.

He injected the freezing liquid into the back of her right hip (the iliac crest) and then prodding around gently, he assessed for numbness. She said she didn't feel anything. He picked up a large bore needle, and injected it into the same area. As he twisted the needle deliberately and resolutely, he asked her to shout "pain" when she felt it. Without moving or wincing, she shouted the word twice. He would then reposition the needle. She gripped Aisling's hands, grimacing now and then, while I rubbed the back of her head. We both talked to her.

I felt like I was freezing up inside when the needle made a crunching noise inside the bone, like a nail going through a plaster wall. After Nebojsa extracted the syringe full of bone marrow, he handed it to the lab technician who took care of the processing.

On Tuesday morning, the doctors came on rounds.

Finally some good news. The MRI report showed that Deirdre's brain was clear of leukemic cells or lesions. Deirdre looked relieved as she nodded at Dr. White and said, "That's really good."

Nebojsa told her that she would be having a lumbar puncture (LP) that afternoon. This was to test for leukemic cells in the spinal fluid and to inject a chemo drug into the fluid.

The transfusions and IV fluids had increased her energy level. After the doctors left, she sat on the blue armchair and read for a while. She was reading a book on China—she varied her reading material between books and fashion magazines.

On Wednesday morning, April 9, Nebojsa encouraged us to pay a visit to the third floor.

"You'll be surprised what you'll see down there," he said.

He wouldn't tell us what it was.

Deirdre was curious. After Donna found us a wheelchair and Deirdre put a disposable face mask around her mouth and nose, Aisling and I wheeled her down the corridor and took the elevators down to the third floor. We arrived and walked to the left and found an aquarium—Nebojsa's surprise—that contained artificial coral and plants, with yellow, red, and green fish swimming in different directions.

Deirdre took her mask off and got up from the wheelchair to stand and gaze at the fish. She loved the ocean and the life in it and had taken scuba diving lessons as a teenager. However, for the past five years salt water had aggravated the eczema rash. It gave her a burning sensation that prevented her from swimming in the sea.

We stayed for about fifteen minutes and took some pictures before Deirdre put the mask back on and we went back upstairs.

At noon, Nebojsa arrived to do the lumbar puncture. During the procedure, Deirdre sat on the side of the bed, leaning forward over a bedside table, her feet resting on a stool so that the spine curved, giving easier access to the area between the disks. Aisling and I stood facing her, holding her hands. After freezing the area, Nebojsa injected a small needle into one of the soft spots between the spinal disks (vertebrae) in her lower back. He withdrew a small amount of fluid into a syringe and sent it to the lab for testing. He then injected a potent chemotherapy drug, Methotrexate, into the spinal fluid. Methotrexate would kill any leukemic cells that infiltrated the spinal fluid.

Deirdre—apart from squeezing our hands—didn't budge throughout the procedure. To prevent any bleeding from the needle site and to avoid headaches, she had to lie flat on her back for a few hours afterward.

Ann and Deirdre by the fish tank—April 9, 2008

Chapter 6

CHEMOTHERAPY BEGINS

**Courage is to feel the daily daggers of relentless
steel and keep on living.—Douglas Malloch**

Later in the afternoon, Deirdre was taken by stretcher to the radiology
department on the third floor for the insertion of a special IV called a hickman
line. She lay on the stretcher in the waiting room and gazed out through the
wall-to-wall window at the blue sky, a plaintive look on her face.

"I can't wait to have this treatment over with so I can go out to the beach,"
she said. She wore a blue hospital gown and had her hair tied up in a ponytail.
Her slightly swollen face was a pasty grey colour. She said she felt nervous
about the procedure, despite my assurances that she wouldn't feel anything
after she was given medication to sedate her.

Five minutes after our arrival, a nurse emerged from the X-ray room.
She was tall and dark-haired; her name was Kelly. Around the same time the
radiologist, Dr. Peter, arrived from outside, carrying a backpack across his
shoulder. Deirdre had met him before; he was one of Aisling's tutors. Kelly and
Peter put Deirdre at ease. They asked her about Japan and about the dancing she
used to do. Deirdre seemed to forget her fears as she answered their questions.

"This will take about twenty to thirty minutes," Peter said, assuming a
matter-of-fact air to help Deirdre relax. "You won't feel any pain. We'll give
you some sedation, and before you know it you'll be on your way." He went
on to explain the procedure. He would make two tiny incisions, one in her
lower neck and one in her right upper chest, and insert the hickman line into
a large vein, using special X-ray equipment to help him guide the line into the
vein. On completion, he would suture the line to her upper chest to prevent
it from coming out.

We told Deirdre we'd wait outside before they pushed her stretcher in through the large door of the X-ray room.

The X-ray room was filled with high-tech equipment, colourful monitors, X-ray machines, and computers that hung from ceilings and walls. Nurses, doctors, and technicians were busy doing procedures and checking patients' information on the monitors.

While we waited, Aisling and I chatted and read information leaflets on the hickman line. Thirty minutes later Peter emerged, walking alongside Deirdre's stretcher. He told us that everything went well.

Deirdre was extremely drowsy and comfortable looking as we accompanied her back to her room.

The hickman line had three soft white lumens or tubes that hung from the insertion site on Deirdre's chest. Each lumen had a port at the end of it. Transfusions, drugs, and IV fluids would be given through the ports. One lumen was reserved for taking blood samples. The line prevented numerous needle pokes and it could stay in for years.

Deirdre, fearful it might become dislodged, protected it like it was her lifeline, holding onto the lumens even when she slept. When she finally realized it was encased securely she ignored it and treated it like another body appendage. She said that it made her feel like the Borg (the *Star Trek* half human–half robot).

On Wednesday morning, the doctors and nurses came on rounds. Dr. White smiled at Deirdre as he walked to the foot of the bed. He asked her how she felt. She gave him a half-smile. I could sense her terror while she waited for the results of the bone marrow biopsy.

Aisling and I stood on either side of the bed and held her hands. To stop her hand from trembling, she gripped onto mine as if she were about to fall into a deep, dark hole.

My heart pounded against my chest wall. In a caring and soft-spoken manner, Dr. White began to explain the results of the bone marrow biopsy. His uneasiness was palpable as he stood at the end of the bed. There were eight people in the room. Apprehension permeated the atmosphere.

"You have both types of acute leukemia," he said. "Myeloid and lymphoblastic, which is very unusual. You have a larger percentage of myeloid." Deirdre squeezed my hand tighter, and I could sense her body shaking.

"Each type will have to be treated separately," he continued. "The drug regimens are different for each type. Each drug is very potent and can cause toxicity to the organs, so only one type of the leukemia can be treated at a time. This means two rounds of chemo. We will begin treatment for the myeloid type today. You will need a bone marrow transplant after both types are in remission." Looking at Aisling and Conor, he asked if they would donate their bone marrow and without hesitation, they both answered yes.

Toward the end, he said, "I'm sorry." We had no idea what he alluded to. He continued with more explanations and asked if we had any questions.

Deirdre, sitting on top of the bed, looked confused and terrified. She was silent, and what little colour there was in her face drained away. I asked about the duration of this round of treatment. The chemo drugs would be given over eight days. She would remain in hospital for about two weeks after that.

"I am going ahead and looking toward a cure," he added, as he turned to leave the room.

This last statement gave us hope; we grasped it and held on tight. It allowed us the freedom to enjoy precious moments with one another as we looked forward to a full recovery and to getting our little planet back on course.

After the team left the room, Deirdre looked at me with wide, frightened-looking eyes.

"I feel like I'm freaking out," she said, her voice raspy and laced with apprehension. "And why did he say he was sorry?"

"He said that because you need two rounds of chemotherapy," I answered in a calm, firm voice, trying desperately to set her mind at ease. "Concentrate on what he said about a cure. I know you're freaked out. Just think ahead to three months' time when you'll have the chemo over with." After half an hour, she decided she was overreacting and then relaxed.

Throughout my nursing career I never felt the compulsion to explore information on leukemia. That was a blessing and, I'm sure, my ignorance was "meant to be." It left me blissfully unaware of the dismal prospects for Deirdre's survival.

Full of hope, I took things day by day, influencing Deirdre with my optimism, while she adhered meticulously to medical advice, intent on getting well enough to return to Japan, and to continue on with her life and her dreams.

Early on Wednesday afternoon, April 9, Donna came into the room and told Deirdre that she would be given the chemo drugs in a few hours. At first Deirdre was reticent and embarrassed about her fear. After a few minutes she put her hands against the side of her face.

"I'm scared," she said, looking at Donna. "I know I have to have it, but I'm so afraid something weird will happen to me."

Donna put her arm around her shoulder.

"We can give you medication for any pain or discomfort that you might have," she said softly. After a little while, Deirdre sat back against the pillows and looked more relaxed.

"I'm getting more psyched up for it. The sooner it starts, the sooner it'll be over with," she said.

Ten minutes later, Conor arrived with Tim Hortons tea and biscuits from the coffee shop on the first floor. While we drank the tea and ate the biscuits, spread with raspberry jam, Conor tried to cheer Deirdre up.

"You get to eat in bed, Deirdre, while we have to sit on these hard chairs," he quipped, as Deirdre picked the crumbs from the sheet.

"Got to have some benefits."

Around 3:30 that afternoon, Donna gave Deirdre some Tylenol, IV Gravol, and a steroid pill to prevent some of the side effects of the chemo drugs. A five-day course of Allopurinol was started to help prevent kidney damage.

At 4:00 PM Donna and another nurse came to begin the chemo treatment. They carried two bags of IV fluid. One was covered by a dark plastic bag; it had the chemo drug Daunorubicin in it. It took about thirty minutes to go through the IV line. Another IV bag containing Cytarabine would run continuously for seven days. After checking the bags' labels with the label on Deirdre's arm bracelet, Donna threaded the IV tubing through the cassettes in the IV pumps and connected them to the ports of the hickman line. After she pressed a few buttons on the pump, the fluid began to course through Deirdre's veins.

Deirdre kept looking at Daichi's picture, keeping her eyes away from the paraphernalia to the right of her. Aisling and I held her hands. Donna stayed for fifteen minutes, watching for any initial side effects, chatting with Deirdre and putting her at ease.

"*Phew.* I'm so relieved that's over with," Deirdre said when the fifteen minutes ended and there were no side effects. She had cleared the first hurdle.

Deirdre and Conor—August 1991

Chapter 7
BONE MARROW DONATION

**Life is a comedy to those who think and a tragedy
to those who feel.—Horatio Walpole**

One day, we talked again about the side effects of the chemo. Hair loss was least among Deirdre's concerns.

"Oh, I'm not worried about that," she said, shrugging her shoulders impassively. "I'll find a nice hat to wear, and it will grow back. I'm more worried about the nausea, those mouth sores that everybody talks about, and the organ damage."

Deirdre's attitude would not surprise anyone who knew her. Always very much her own person and unconcerned about other people's opinions, she lived life her way. She loved fashion and style and indulged herself with nice clothes, shoes, purses, makeup, and whatever she could afford—and sometimes what she could not afford. This wasn't to impress others, but to please herself. Assertive and compassionate, she disliked facades and very quickly saw their transparency. She was sometimes introspective—evidenced by her diary entries which showed how insightful she was about the ups and downs of life.

After a couple days in hospital, the hair on the back of her head was tangled like a bird's nest. Aisling and I took on the challenging task of washing it every other day. To wash it, Deirdre lay flat on her back in bed, her head resting over a plastic trough that narrowed into a channel at the end. Aisling would pour a jug of water over Deirdre's head. The water flowed directly from the trough into a bucket that sat on the floor by the side of the bed. Because of Deirdre's discomfort lying flat, we had to work swiftly; sometimes it took us less than five minutes.

One day after we had dried her hair and helped her onto the armchair, she patted her hair and said, "I feel like a princess with all this attention."

Early menopause was another side effect of the chemo drugs. This information jolted Deirdre. Thoughts of it preyed on her mind for a couple of days. I felt like she was being hurled forward into the vintage of middle age, robbed of young womanhood, like a tree losing its leaves in the middle of summer.

The inability to bear children didn't concern her as much as the hot flashes. She saw those as belonging to someone older—like her mother. I felt sad for her but encouraged her to look at the positive side.

"It doesn't happen to everyone, Deirdre," I said. "Try to think about getting through the treatment. You can deal with that later."

She talked to Daichi on the phone about it. She said that he was very supportive and more concerned about her recovery, telling her they could adopt if they wanted children. Discussing it with him seemed to put her mind at ease.

Before Daichi came along, Deirdre had no desire to marry. One day a couple of years before, she, Aisling, and I were out for a drive. We were talking about marriage. I sat in the back, Deirdre in the passenger seat, and Aisling in the driver's seat.

"Marriage and a wedding is so *you*, Aisling," Deirdre said, leaning over to look at Aisling. "But definitely not for me. I'd be blushing all the way down the aisle. Oh no, I'll never get married."

When she met Daichi her plans changed.

Aisling visited at least twice a day, and more whenever Deirdre was having any procedures. The university staff was very empathetic and they made allowances for her absence when she needed to be with Deirdre. Sometimes I noticed the concern on Aisling's face and saw tension in the corner of her eyes, especially when things weren't going well with Deirdre. Amidst it all, she made every effort to lighten things up, bringing Deirdre news of their friends and sharing anecdotes with her. They were always extremely close and few explanations were necessary between them.

On Thursday, April 18, Nebojsa brought disappointing news. I had gone home for an hour while Conor visited. When I arrived back, Deirdre was sitting upright in bed, tears flowing down her face. Conor sat on a chair beside her.

"What's going on, Deirdre?" I asked, sitting on the bed and putting my arm around her shoulder.

"Conor and Aisling can't be donors," she cried. "The doctor said they didn't match. I don't know what's going to happen now. He said something about finding some other donors. Am I a freak or something? First I have these two kinds of leukemia. That's unusual, and now I have weird bone marrow."

"It's not unusual for siblings to be incompatible," I said, trying with great difficulty to sound optimistic. "There's certain to be a donor for you in this great big world. You're not *that* unique. It will be another four months before you can have the transplant, so there's lots of time to find one." It took another fifteen minutes to calm her. I tried to portray an air of composure and kept my voice even, my breathing slow, hiding the extent of my own utter disappointment.

The doctors had tried to explain the global list of organ transplants to her, but she understood very little. She was too shocked to absorb any information.

She was added to the global list of bone marrow transplants. This is an international registry where unrelated donors and recipients register for a bone marrow matching. With an unrelated donor, the match would have to be absolutely pristine.

Deirdre's and Aisling's friends and cousins all offered to donate their bone marrow. Aisling's classmates organized a bone marrow donor drive at the medical school. Dr. White said the chances of cousins being compatible donors had the same odds as winning the lottery. The global list was the best alternative after siblings.

When I told Donna about Deirdre's concern, she talked to her and gave her reassurance. Then she called the transplant coordinator nurse who came and explained the transplant process. Her explanations about the abundance of worldwide donors gave Deirdre confidence and hope again.

Monday's X-ray showed a pneumonia and fungal infection in her lungs. The infectious disease specialists came to see her and started her on antifungal pills; the IV antibiotic was taking care of the pneumonia.

Pain around her left sinus was beginning to bother her a lot. The doctor figured she caught something on the plane. Every four to six hours, for fifteen minutes, she was given a saline mist through an oxygen mask, which relieved the sinus pain and the mouth dryness. While the mask covered her mouth and nose and the mist hissed and floated around inside, she sat upright in bed or on the chair, watching TV or reading.

Half-empty cans of soda water and bottled water, a picture of her and Daichi, notepaper, and books cluttered the bedside table. Aquafina was one of several bottled waters that were tested by the hospital lab. It was the only one that was deemed pure enough for consumption by patients with weakened immune systems. Deirdre hoped to prevent mouth sores, so she brushed her teeth several times a day. She rinsed her mouth afterwards with the club soda the hospital provided, and recommended, as a mouthwash.

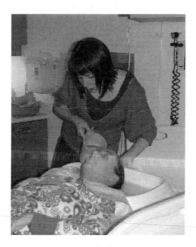

Aisling washing Deirdre's hair—April 2008.

Chapter 8
SETTLING INTO HOSPITAL

Let loose of what you can't control. Serenity will be yours. --Unknown

At night, the room was in semidarkness, lit only by a night light. The rhythmic drone of the four IV pumps that pushed the fluid and medications along Deirdre's veins was magnified by the silence, broken now and then by one pump's beep, signalling a medication or fluid bag had run through.

During the first week, Deirdre pushed the nurse's call bell as soon as the beep went off, but as she got used to the sound, she slept through, leaving me to call. The nurse came right away. She was guided past the doorway by a beam of light from a flashlight that she held in her hand. After she pushed a few buttons and adjusted the flow of the IV, she asked if we needed anything. Then she left. Now, whenever I hear the sound of the same pumps where I work, it transports me back to those nights filled with hope for Deirdre's recovery.

At night, I tossed and turned in my half-sleep. The intermittent footsteps of the nurses outside the room and the sound of their soft voices had a soothing effect. Some nights, the level of activity noticeably increased when a new patient was admitted.

During Deirdre's first five days in hospital, my own weight dropped eight pounds. Despite frequent short periods of meditation, I felt stuffed with worry. Looking back, I recognize this sudden shift of the pendulum of fate affected me more than I realized.

On the first Friday after Deirdre arrived, Aisling stayed overnight with her. I finally felt confident about leaving. Chemo was underway, making its assault on the leukemic cells. Deirdre was experiencing no major side effects. Aisling gave me strict instructions not to show up until 10:00 the next morning.

"We will call if you are needed," she said forcefully.

"And make yourself a nice drink," Deirdre added, a luminous smile on her face. She was happy to hang out with Aisling; they planned to watch a DVD movie.

When I got home, I poured myself an ounce of brandy—my Irish mother's cure for all ailments. Other than for medicinal purposes, she never drank alcohol. After I forced the brandy down, I reached in the fridge and got a large bowl of the leftover meat and vegetable stew. I heated it up, added butter and HP sauce, and ate every morsel.

Just as I finished, a friend of mine, aware of my plans to stay home for the night, arrived at my door. Her arms cradled a warm blueberry pie covered with a dish towel. The pie had just come out of the oven.

We sat on the tall, slim bamboo chairs that stood in front of the island in the kitchen. While we drank tea and ate slices of pie covered with whipped cream, we chatted. I recounted the happenings of the past few days. As we talked, I felt my body relax like I'd come in from a blizzard. My friend left around 10:00 PM, telling me to call her if I needed anything.

After she left, I walked upstairs to the bathroom, filled the claw-footed bathtub, added fragrant bath salts, and spent twenty minutes luxuriously soaking in the warm water. Later, I lay in bed looking through the window at the night sky speckled with stars. A bright moon glowed between the bare black branches of the maple tree. I thanked my spirit for helping us this far. Then, relishing the silence, I drifted into a deep, undisturbed sleep.

At 8:00 am, when I opened my eyes, the early morning light had already brightened up the room. My thoughts were filled with optimism for Deirdre's recovery. I made my way down to the kitchen, pulled the frying pan from the cupboard, and made eggs and bacon. The sizzling sound and the bacon smell were soothing, reassuring me that life would one day be back to normal. I sat at the counter and had tea and toast with the bacon and eggs.

I called Deirdre around 9:00 am. She answered right away and sounded in good spirits.

"We watched the movie that Ben brought in," she said. "I went to sleep around 11:30 and slept pretty well. I barely heard the pumps beep. I had to call for codeine pills once for a headache, but after about ten minutes I was asleep again."

Aisling sounded exhausted.

"I'm so tired," she said. "I didn't sleep a wink."

Before I walked back to the hospital I called Esther, my sister in Ireland. She was delighted when I called and told her that Deirdre was handling the chemo well. She planned to visit in a few weeks when Deirdre was out of hospital.

The previous January, I had discovered some rotten shingles around my house. On Thursday the contractor called. He finally had time to repair the shingles. I told him to go ahead, hoping everything would be completed before Deirdre came home from hospital.

Most mornings, at 7:00 am, when Deirdre was in hospital and sleeping, I walked home for an hour. The contractor would arrive on time to have a quick discussion about the work. On the first morning, as I was leaving to return to the hospital, he shook his head, looking at the rotten shingles as if a great tragedy had occurred.

Shrugging my shoulders, I said, "Believe me, this is very trivial," and walked away. Dealing with the work on the house, something positive, was a welcome distraction from the all-encompassing illness.

On a beautiful sunny day, nine days into chemo treatment, Deirdre was at her worst. After a quick visit home, I was about to return to the hospital. I stood across the street and looked back at my cream-coloured house with the flat roof.

The front door—Deirdre had painted it an orangey red a few years before—had been removed. The wooden frame around it was black and rotten. Looking at it, I saw it as a metaphor for my life; a life falling apart all around me. A few days later, the wooden frame was replaced and a new door put in. I found solace in the analogy that Deirdre would soon have that rotten disease removed, and new bone marrow implanted.

Normally, I rarely stayed at home for long. Before Deirdre's illness, I needed to go here and there, frequent the local coffee shop and catch up on the news in town, go to movies, to an occasional play, and to whatever else was going on. But now, it was as if my old self had walked away. An uncanny feeling of peaceful surrender engulfed my whole being when I sat with Deirdre. At those times I was oblivious to any tomorrows, to what went on outside her room. I didn't think about what might happen. *Today is all there is, and Deirdre is here beside me.* Whenever any worry or anxiety tried to grab me, I prayed and relaxed again.

During the day, the hubbub of the hospital was constant. Each morning at about 7:30, the place came to life with an array of staff that came and went. The nurses and doctors discussed patients' progress at the nursing station. Specialists and entourages of medical staff walked alongside one another, teaching and learning, using their expertise to solve specific problems and to heal ailments. Periodically, Nebojsa's spirited voice resonated above it all.

Cleaners, porters, kitchen staff, and technicians all played their roles in the chain of patient care. The sound of the rubber wheels of stretchers and wheelchairs transporting patients, the clanking of food trays placed onto trolleys, laundry carts pushed and pulled—all added to the life of the place.

The racket continued until around 5:00 PM, when the bulk of staff left for home. Visitors arrived in larger numbers after supper, creating somewhat of a family atmosphere as they chatted about their day's activities and other news. At 10:00 PM, after the lights in the corridors were dimmed, a hushed silence prevailed.

Aisling was visiting one afternoon, two days after chemo began. I took the opportunity to get away from the hospital for a little while and I walked home. While I was away Deirdre had a panic attack, precipitated by a combination of Benadryl and another medication, which caused a flood of adrenalin. It happened as I was on my way back from the hospital and the nurses couldn't get hold of me.

When I walked into the room, Deirdre was shaking with terror. She was sitting upright against pillows and looking around, her eyes wide. Aisling held her hand and tried to soothe her. I ran and sat beside her on the bed. "Take deep breaths, Deirdre," I urged. "You're okay and everything's going to be fine."

I squeezed her shoulder gently. Five minutes later she calmed down. After that incident, I decided it was time to purchase a cell phone.

"Daichi is amazed that you don't have a cell phone," Deirdre had said one day, with a big grin on her face.

"Well, tell him I know the location of most pay phones here in Halifax and I do have a house phone," I said defensively. She explained to him why I didn't own one, but he still thought I was in the dark ages. In Japan, I'd noticed that most of the population talked incessantly on cell phones, except on trains where phones were required to be on mute and could not be used.

Everybody was happy when I finally succumbed, and moved ahead into the year 2008 by purchasing a cell phone. At first I had difficulty adjusting the volume, but after a week of entering and leaving the hospital and having to alternate the volume from high to vibrate, I became adept at it. Texting was still out of the question. Deirdre showed me a compartment in my purse that was designated for a cell phone and that pocket saved a lot of rummaging.

Deirdre continued to eat like a bird. Most mornings, when I returned to her room from my walk home, the breakfast tray sat untouched on the bedside table. After I coaxed her to eat something, she would put a dab of butter on a bran muffin, pick at it, and wash it down with a few mouthfuls of cranberry juice. She refused the little carton of Ensure that came with each meal. I brought her cans of chocolate Boost, which she liked, from Shoppers Drug Mart, but the most she could drink was half a can. Despite regular anti-nausea medication, she continued to have bouts of queasiness.

She craved various food items from her favourite eating places in Halifax.

We brought in her flavour of the day: goat cheese pizza covered with bacon, red peppers, and red onions from the Argyle Bar & Grill, pita from the Pita Pit Deli, a club sandwich from the Bluenose restaurant, potato and broccoli mixture from a fast food place close by, and a sundae from Dairy Queen.

Reese's Peanut Butter Cups were her all-time favourite chocolates.

I worried when her daily weight was checked, partly because of weight loss, but also because of the anxiety she experienced after she was weighed.

"I'm getting so skinny," she would say, a disconcerted look on her face, as she stepped from the scales. She had never concerned herself about putting on weight, resisting the idea of slimness as "the way to look."

"You'll put it on again when you come home," I said, trying to console her. She would sigh and nod her head in agreement, but still looked unconvinced.

She was given high volumes of fluids. This meant frequent trips to the washroom, especially at night. I woke up whenever she moved, and when I saw her feet heading to the floor, I jumped up beside her. After I pulled the IV pump's plug from the socket on the wall behind the bed, I put my arm behind her tiny back. I supported her while she walked to the bathroom, pushing the IV pole in front. After we manoeuvred our way past the narrow doorway of the washroom, I waited outside, my hand on the doorknob, ready to charge in should I hear any unusual noise. After a while, I settled down and stopped worrying about her potential head injury.

Once, as we walked back from the washroom, I had a sudden flashback to a time when I walked my mother, now deceased, from the washroom in the old farmhouse to her bed. As I held onto Deirdre's arm, I could feel my mother's energy so strongly that, for a few seconds, I thought it was her beside me—it was like déjà vu, but more profound. A sense of panic gripped me. I was terrified that this was a harbinger of things to come.

After I settled Deirdre back to bed, I made an excuse to use the washroom down the corridor. I went to the kitchen, sat with my elbows on the table, my face in my hands, and took some deep breaths. After a few minutes, I relaxed enough to return to Deirdre's bedside.

Deirdre eating Reese's Peanut Butter Cups—April 2008

Chapter 9

VISITORS

Hope is the physician of every misery. —Irish proverb

As I walked home each morning I savoured the crisp spring air and felt full of life and hope. On drizzly days the moist air was refreshing. The branches on the trees were mostly bare, but a few buds were starting to show here and there. In some flower beds along the way, crocuses peeked above the ground, displaying their dark purple petals and green leaves.

Throughout most of the walk I was oblivious to the busy morning traffic and the clusters of high school students who walked past me, going in the opposite direction. I would just zigzag around them to get by.

As I walked, I prayed and meditated—asked for Deirdre's continued healing and for the strength and faith to continue to surrender to my spirit.

Prepared for the occasional rainy day, I had an array of colourful umbrellas: purple, yellow, green, and blue. I kept two in Deirdre's room, one at home, and one in the car. I had bought them at Wal-Mart before we went to Japan. Before travelling there, Deirdre had advised us to bring umbrellas as sun protection. These were ideal. They had insulated lining, and were a godsend, especially in Kyoto where the heat was an unrelenting, humid 38°C.

By Sunday, April 13, four days after chemo started, there were no major side effects other than bouts of nausea and headaches . Every day, Dr. White dropped in on rounds, and after he evaluated Deirdre, he delivered an update on her progress. Blood results showed that her major organs were tolerating the chemo drugs. The blood cell levels were going in the right direction. Down.

Each morning around 5:00 AM, while Deirdre slept, a nurse slipped quietly into the room. Without turning the light on, and with practised ease, she drew blood samples from a port in the hickman line. When chemo treatment began, the nurses recorded the daily blood results on a sheet of paper and pinned it on the bulletin board. Each day, we waited eagerly to see the numbers on the paper. The blood cell levels continued to decrease as hoped, while the chemo drugs continued their attack with their "killer rays."

As expected, the good white blood cells, the red cells, and platelets were also being destroyed. The white cells would rejuvenate after the effects of the chemo wore off, and weren't vital right now. But the risk of infection was extremely high without the army of white cells to do battle against infections. When the platelets and red cells dropped to a certain level, Deirdre needed transfusions of both. She required platelets about every two to three days and red cells about twice a week. Sometimes she received a "single donor" platelet transfusion that increased her platelet count considerably more than the "universal" platelets. The process of donating "single donor" platelets takes about two hours of the donor's time, compared to fifteen minutes of giving whole blood, from which "universal" platelets are extracted. Deirdre and I talked about how grateful we felt to all donors, especially those who donated the two hours of their time to give the single donor platelets.

In the first few days after her admission, two big hives appeared on one of her legs following a platelet transfusion. From then on, she was given the antihistamine Benadryl before every transfusion. She grew to savour its relaxation effects.

"I just feel so out of it," she would say after the nurse injected it into the IV line. As the Benadryl flowed through her veins, her eyelashes fluttered before she closed her eyes and she glided into a deep, short sleep. Sometimes Conor teased her about it.

"So Deirdre, are you getting the Benadryl high today?"

"Just waiting to be surprised."

Most days she dressed in beige, fuchsia, and floral knee-length nightgowns with shorts that came to her knees. She wore hospital gowns during tests and procedures. We brought her a pillow and fleece blanket from home. The nurses encouraged us to bring in whatever would enhance her comfort.

Every few days, I took her laundry home. The nurses advised me to wash Deirdre's clothes separate from the regular laundry at home. Deirdre's clothing could still be contaminated with biohazardous chemo-drug residue.

The Manorapid hand-washing liquid, which smelled like alcohol, killed 90 percent of germs. I became obsessed with it. After I squirted the liquid from the green container onto a paper towel, I rubbed it onto every horizontal surface, the outside of water bottles and soda cans, bedrails, the call button, pump buttons, the string attached to the light switch behind the bed, book covers, and whatever I laid my eyes on. Sometimes the room reeked, but it kept the germs away. I was determined to shield Deirdre from every one of them. Sometimes she teased me about it.

"This is the Manorapid queen," she would say to others in the room, as I tried to swab another surface unobtrusively. While Deirdre was in the hospital for the second round of chemo, my obsession had worn off. I had more confidence in her ability to fight the bugs.

"I liked it better when you were cleaning more," she said one day. "I could still catch something." I took up the task again to keep her happy, but lacked the same enthusiasm.

She was happy to have news of her illness broadcast via Facebook, etc.; however, news of how much she suffered was prohibited territory to everyone except the family and Daichi. She very effectively let me know her wishes.

One day, shortly after chemo started, she was lying on her side, a wet facecloth over her forehead, her eyes closed. The headache and nausea were worse than usual. The phone on the bedside table rang and I picked it up after one ring. It was one of her friends and she asked to speak to Deirdre.

"I'm afraid she's having a bad day today and she's too sick to talk," I explained apologetically. "But I'll ask her to call you later on." When I put the phone down, Deirdre turned to face me.

"You shouldn't have told her I was having a bad day. I don't want anyone thinking I'm depressed," she said, fixing me with a direct look.

"I meant you were having a bad day, physically," I clarified.

"Well, they'll take it I'm depressed and take pity on me. I'm not some sort of victim." After that, when she felt too sick to talk to anyone, I either unplugged the phone or told whoever called that she was resting.

Deirdre got fearful and irritated if we regarded her too often or for any length of time.

"I'm not an artifact in a museum," she would say.

If we weren't talking to her, we had to occupy ourselves with reading, watching TV, using the computer, or talking to one another. Whenever I worried about some side effect, such as sores in her mouth or on her lips, I had to steal a quick peek from the corner of my eye—I had to look "without looking."

When she was free of pain and nausea, Deirdre enjoyed having Conor around.

"I like having Conor around," she would say, a smirk on her face. "He just sits there with the computer and lifts his head once in a while to make some funny cynical remark. He's easy to boss around as well."

Conor and Deirdre had a unique relationship. It was entertaining to listen to them banter back and forth as they used quick-witted remarks.

"How come you always have money, Conor?" Deirdre would ask him.

"Because I don't spend it on clothes and booze like you and Aisling," he would answer.

Even as a child Deirdre had the ability to keep everybody entertained. One day when she was seven years old, she wanted to have a friend over after school. I agreed, on condition that Conor could play with them. He was four years old, at home all day, and looking forward to having Deirdre to play with when she came home. Deirdre was happy with this arrangement.

After they had been playing a while, I noticed Conor crouched on his hands and knees outside the bedroom door. Ten minutes later, when I looked again, he was still in the same position. I asked him what he was doing there.

"Deirdre told me to stay here," he said, looking up at me, smiling. "I'm a dog."

I went into the bedroom. Deirdre and her friend Adrienne were sitting on the floor, chatting to one another, happily brushing a doll's hair.

"How come you're not playing with Conor," I asked them, "and why is he outside the door?"

"We're playing house," Deirdre answered, looking up at me, her eyes wide and serious looking. "Conor is the dog and he's protecting the house."

Two days after arriving home from Japan, word of her illness got around via phone, e-mails, and the international electronic bulletin board Facebook. Numerous get-well cards kept arriving. Posters and drawings sent by her friends lined the walls and windowsills in her room. Flowers were banned because they could carry bugs and bacteria that could be lethal to an immune-compromised patient. Three helium balloons floated above the bedside cupboard.

Deirdre got e-mails from relatives and acquaintances, many of whom she hadn't heard from in a long time. For short blocks of time, when she felt well enough, she clattered away on her laptop keyboard, sitting on top of the bed, legs outstretched.

I got messages from relatives in Australia and Boston who work in medicine. They assured me that the Victoria General Hospital in Halifax was one of the best leukemia treatment centres in the world. I was already aware of that and thankful that Deirdre was there.

Deirdre attracted loyal and steadfast friends. On weekends, her friends April Clyburne-Sherin and Aisling Chin-Yee came by train or plane from Montreal to see her. During their first weekend they only saw her for twenty minutes, but they returned the following weekend.

Throughout most of the hospital stay, she received very few visitors other than family; fifteen minutes of animated conversation sapped her strength.

Whenever she did see anybody, she quickly veered the conversation away from her ailments, asking them about themselves. She designated her friend Graeme as her personal secretary. Aisling would call him with updates on Deirdre's progress and when she could see people, he would relay that message to their circle of friends.

Her friends in Japan sent messages, mainly through e-mail. Some of her four- to six-year-old Japanese students sent her get-well notes and drawings by mail. Marie Verlingo, a recruiting director for the company Deirdre worked with, not only looked after Deirdre's affairs in Japan, but was also a very good friend of Deirdre's. She was full of concern for her and passed messages back and forth between Deirdre and her working colleagues there.

Marie sent a copy of the weekly newsletter from Deirdre's workplace. It was called the *Weekly Message*. Her boss, Jack Stern, submitted this article to the newsletter the week Deirdre left Japan.

It is all too often easy for us to become overly absorbed with the relatively minor intricacies of our lives. We may often see what are in reality "the inconveniences of life" as earth-shaking dramas or waves of calamitous events or misfortunes. We sometimes need to be reminded that there are realities that put in perspective what is truly important in life and what are truly life-altering events. These perspective moments bring us clarity, awareness, and reflecting humility, usually due at the numbing expense of someone near and dear to us. We are therefore reminded how humbling and fragile our lives can be, and return to a more humane and caring sense of ourselves and more significantly the connections we share with those around us. For those of you who know Deirdre Porter, there are not enough words to describe how truly good a person she is, and how deeply saddened and stunned we all feel by this news. Deirdre left an indelible impression on all of us at ALS [the company] as a caring and devoted teacher, a kind and trusted friend, and as a conscientious and selfless individual—we will greatly miss seeing her and will be fervently praying for her recovery.

Dave Gracey, who Deirdre referred to as "my best friend in Tokyo," was also a teacher in Tokyo. He grew up in Vancouver. According to Deirdre, they went back and forth to work on the train together. Deirdre said Dave used to make her laugh all the time they travelled together. They were constantly poking fun at one another.

A few weeks before she came home, when Deirdre complained every day about not feeling well, Dave teased her about becoming a hypochondriac. She felt that deep down he worried about her. While she was in the hospital, Dave sent e-mails that, she said, she found comical and uplifting.

Daichi stored some of her belongings in Dave's apartment after she left. There were numerous shoes among them. Dave teased her about the shoes.

"I'm going to sell all your shoes, Deirdre," he wrote in one e-mail that she showed me. "I'll keep all the money for me—to buy painkillers like you have. I wouldn't want to be left out. I hope everything is going well and that you'll soon be back and destroying the common good throughout civilized society. How long until this is over? I really, really miss you and I don't want to have to travel to that godforsaken part of Canada to see you; it's no place for brothers like me to live."

"Don't sell my shoes. I'll kill you. I will hire a hit man if I need to," she had replied.

Aisling Chin Yee and April visiting—April 12, 2008.

Deirdre, Ann, and Aisling (holding one of the umbrellas) atop a hill in Miyajima Island, Japan—July 2007

Chapter *10*

HEALING THERAPIES

**I steer my bark with hope in the head, leaving fear astern.
My hopes indeed sometimes fail, but not oftener than
the forebodings of the gloomy. —Thomas Jefferson**

On April 16, seven days after chemo began, Deirdre's left arm and thigh pain subsided. The chemo had eradicated a large number of cancer cells that caused the swelling and pain. Deirdre's face was swollen, a result of the high volume of IV fluid she had received to protect her kidneys.

Despite her afflictions, her spirits were up. Daichi was to arrive on April 18. We all looked forward to his visit. He had renewed his passport the week before and sent Deirdre a picture of it by e-mail—along with the other twice-daily pictures: brushing his teeth, riding the train with a face mask on, having a haircut, eating an ice cream, etc. They phoned each other every day.

The headaches and sinus pain continued to oscillate. Although the morphine drip alleviated much of the pain, she still needed the codeine pills two to three times every twenty-four hours. The nurses gave whatever was prescribed to sustain her comfort; in Deirdre's words, "They gave me whatever I asked for."

Morphine and codeine, both narcotics, caused a considerable slowdown in her digestive system. After taking them for one week, Deirdre became severely constipated and developed acute abdominal pain that lasted two days. In an effort to relieve the pain, she kept getting in and out of bed, sitting on the commode and pushing, to no avail. She would stand on the floor, lean forward over the side of the bed, one hand across her forehead, the other on her stomach, grimacing with the pain.

I worried about an intestinal obstruction so I brought my stethoscope in from home. When there was no one else in the room, I placed it on her abdomen and heard normal intestinal gurgling sounds. It was music to my ears, allaying my fears of an obstruction. This was one of the few occasions when I couldn't resist going back into my nursing mode.

The nurses persuaded Deirdre to take a vile-tasting but very effective laxative, called lactulose, every six hours. It took her fifteen minutes to swallow an ounce of it. After every sip she pressed her lips together, scrunched her eyes closed, reached her hand out, and placed the half-filled plastic medicine cup on the bedside table. Then she gulped down a mouthful of ginger ale. I sat on the bed, trying to coax her to finish the lactulose.

"Oh man, that's so gross," she would say. "Just leave it there and I'll take some more later on." Knowing it would be the last she would take if I did that, I continued to pester her until the medicine cup was empty.

"Just try and swallow it all at once, then it will be over with," I said.

"Yuk! I can't do that," she said, looking at me like I'd asked her to swallow an ounce of poison. "I'd vomit every bit of it."

Finally, after two days, her bowels moved, creating palpable relief for her and for me. Every day after that, I made a bowl of all-bran cereal covered with blueberries, honey, and milk. She ate it with no complaints, preferring that to the dreaded constipation and lactulose alternative.

Once or twice, Conor stayed with Deirdre while Aisling and I did the ten-minute walk down Spring Garden Road to our regular coffee shop, Steve-O-Reno's. The coffee shop has a warm feel to it, with green leaf motifs painted on terracotta walls, six small square wooden tables, three small round tables, a long bench, and purple, straight-back chairs.

We met some of the regulars, and over a coffee and our favourite apricot scones, we caught up on the news. Eager to hear about Deirdre, they were happy when we told them that she continued to do well. Some told stories of relatives who had brain tumours and other forms of cancer, but who were now doing well. It was their way of reassuring us.

Aisling and her friends had planned to leave on April 24, to go to a concert in California for four days. They had made the arrangements months in advance. She was reluctant to leave, but Deirdre and I persuaded her to go, reminding her that Daichi would be here at that time to help out. Deirdre, always the party animal herself, was adamant that she go as planned.

"Don't be crazy," she said, waving her hand. "Go sing, dance, and have a few drinks for me."

A few times, my friend Barbara Harte, a reiki master and head massage therapist, pampered Deirdre with an "Indian Head Massage." For half an hour, Deirdre would lie back and fall asleep while Barbara gently but firmly worked her hands around Deirdre's hair and scalp, stroking and massaging. I found it soothing just to watch from a chair at the foot of the bed.

David Maginley, a Lutheran minister, staff chaplain and therapeutic touch practitioner, visited Deirdre in the first few days after her admission. He stood tall and thin, at six foot six, and had a sense of humour that Deirdre liked. He offered to do a therapeutic touch (TT) session whenever she felt the need. Deirdre, usually leery about having alternative therapies done by someone she didn't know, had a good feeling about David.

"He has a nice relaxing way about him," she said.

Therapeutic touch is a form of energy therapy that can reduce pain and anxiety, and assist with healing. On a few occasions, when Deirdre felt more uptight than usual—like after the panic attack—she sent me off to look for him.

Whenever he did a session, he encouraged me to stay and observe from my chair a few feet away. With his hands a couple of inches above Deirdre's body, he would move them around in a slow, fluid motion, transferring slowly from her head to her feet. When he completed the session, Deirdre would look relaxed with her eyes closed.

We read a notice about an area on the eleventh floor called "the sunshine room." This was a place where cancer patients undergoing chemo treatment could have massage therapy, reiki, therapeutic touch, and reflexology. This unique facility was opened in 2003, and was run by volunteers who were professionally trained in these therapies. Other volunteers looked after the day-to-day organization, and chatted with patients and family. Wigs and scarves were available there, free of charge.

On two occasions, I took Deirdre up to the sunshine room by wheelchair. A painting of a sunflower covered the entrance to the two rooms. One room had royal blue floral curtains, a royal blue couch, three large armchairs, a white coffee table, and two standing lamps that gave it a homey look overall. The other room had shelves displaying wigs, headscarves, and other accessories. Two ladies sat on the armchairs, knitting. While we waited the fifteen minutes for Deirdre's massage, a lady told us that there was always a lineup.

The therapies were done in an adjoining room, just off the main area. On our first visit, Peggy, a professional massage therapist, gave Deirdre a twenty-minute session.

"That was so relaxing," Deirdre said drowsily as I wheeled her back to her room. She slept for an hour afterwards.

On Thursday, April 17, day seven of chemo treatment, the last of the cytarabine drip had floated through Deirdre's veins. The chemo drugs would continue to do battle for another fifteen or sixteen days.

The nurses were slowly stepping down the morphine drip. Each morning they came and pressed a few buttons on the IV pump, adjusting the rate for the day.

Sometimes Deirdre woke up in the middle of the night sweating profusely, her nightgown and bed linen soaked and needing a change. We thought the hot flashes had started and I asked Nebojsa about it.

Unable to understand my Irish accent, he misinterpreted what I said. When I mentioned menopause, he thought I was asking about Deirdre's inability to have children and insinuated there were more pressing issues right now, like her survival. Deirdre was too weak and miserable to clarify my question, but afterwards we laughed about the accent barriers.

I realized later that despite the slow weaning process, the sweating was a symptom of morphine withdrawal, along with the nausea that was exacerbated by the effects of the chemo drugs. She began to twitch a lot in her sleep and sometimes it woke her up. At first I thought she was dreaming but then began to realize it was another sign of morphine withdrawal. The symptoms continued on for a number of days after that.

The illness consumed my life. In the room with Deirdre, I forgot about the world outside. Instead I watched for any change in her, good or bad. I read every page of literature on the treatment protocols and I attended to most of her needs. On rare occasions, I talked to friends and family. People made us leek soup, scones with special herbs, fruit trays, sweets, and other wonderful food that we kept in the kitchen fridge. It was comforting to know that they were all thinking about us.

Chapter 11

Side Effects Peak

**It's faith in something and enthusiasm for something that
makes a life worth living. —Oliver Wendell Holmes**

On Friday, April 18, Deirdre was filled with excitement and anticipation, looking forward to Daichi's visit. His flight was arriving at 10:00 PM. He had sent an e-mail a few days before, assuring me that he wore a face mask when he travelled on the trains in Tokyo. He would also wear one during the plane journey. He planned to shower at my house before going to see Deirdre. The nurses had advised Deirdre against kissing Daichi on the lips because there was a small risk that she still carried carcinogenic contaminants from the chemo drugs. Deirdre explained this to Daichi over the phone. They were eager to comply with medical advice, and said they appreciated being told about it.

Aisling and I washed her hair that afternoon. It was cropped short at that point. Aisling did the brushing and styling. After some deliberation as to which nightgown she should wear, the three of us finally agreed on the beige one with lion prints.

"You'll be able to get a good rest at home tonight," Deirdre said, sitting upright in the bed, ready for Daichi's visit. "Daichi will help me to the bathroom and whatever else I need."

"That's good, Deirdre," I answered, smiling. "I'm sure you guys will manage without me, but call me if you need anything."

Aisling and Conor went to the airport while I stayed with Deirdre. When Aisling called from her cell phone to say they had picked Daichi up and were leaving the airport, I drove home to welcome him.

Around 11:00 PM, Aisling came through the front door into the hallway and Daichi walked behind her. With a bashful smile he extended his hand towards me and gave a solid handshake. His eyes were a velvety dark colour. Oriental-looking, he had high cheekbones and jet-black hair. At about six foot two, he was slender and well built. He refused food or drink, anxious to get down and see Deirdre. After he showered, he sprinted down the stairs, thanked me, and asked Aisling and Conor to drive him to the hospital.

When they left, I wondered what Deirdre's face would look like when she first saw Daichi. Later that night, Aisling called me from her apartment.

"Deirdre looked so happy," she said. "She had a big smile on her face when she saw Daichi. It was so nice to watch them, especially when they hugged one another."

I felt a lot lighter, relieved and happy for Deirdre. Exhausted, I went upstairs to my own bed and after I read for a little while, drifted into an unbroken sleep.

I woke up about 7:00 AM and after I lay there for ten minutes relaxing and praying, I went downstairs and made breakfast. As I spread butter and peach jam onto a slice of toast, I noticed the red light on the phone flashing. I pressed the button to check the messages—there were several from friends and family, all asking about Deirdre. I sat and listened to them while I had tea and toast and a bowl of strawberry yoghurt.

It was after 9:00 AM when I made my way down to the hospital. I put a sandwich, cookies, pita bread, humus, and apples into a large bag and drove down.

When I got to Deirdre's room, Daichi was sitting on a chair by the window reading. He wore a sweatshirt with horizontal black and white stripes, blue jeans, and white sneakers. Deirdre sat upright in bed, dozing. Her breathing was steady and soft. She wore a fuchsia housecoat over the beige nightgown. The atmosphere in the room had a nice calm feel to it.

As soon as I entered, Daichi jumped up. Walking towards me, he greeted me enthusiastically, pulled up a chair, and invited me to sit down. Deirdre opened her eyes. They had a sick look to them, but her face was transformed with a luminous smile when she heard Daichi's voice. The connection between them was palpable.

"How was the night?" I asked.

"It was good," Daichi answered. "I am so happy to be in Halifax with Deirdre. I will stay with her every night," he said, smiling. I liked his accent and the tiny pause between his words.

"Yeah, he helped me to the bathroom," Deirdre piped up, "and he called the nurse when I needed pain and nausea pills. But he hardly slept all night."

"Oh, that's okay," he said, shrugging his shoulders. "I can have a nap later today."

We chatted for a short time. Daichi talked about the journey here, and told me about his family in Japan—about his brother and a sister. He said his father worked in Tokyo, travelling back and forth to their home in Osaka on the weekends. His mother, like most Japanese mothers, didn't work outside the home.

After a while, I went downstairs to the first floor and bought Tim Hortons coffee for Daichi and me, and tea and a cheese biscuit for Deirdre. Daichi sat on a chair by the window and drank the coffee and ate the tomato and ham sandwich that I had made. I had an oatmeal raisin cookie with my coffee. Deirdre sat upright on the bed, sipping her tea and picking away at the biscuit. She had a contented look on her face, as though she looked forward to a long and healthy life with Daichi.

During Daichi's visit, I continued to spend a good part of the day with Deirdre. I wanted to stay abreast of what was happening so I tried to be present for doctors' rounds, specialists' visits, and any tests or procedures. Deirdre wanted me to listen in on any updates because new information scared her. She relied on me to grasp the information, and to ask the appropriate questions.

While Daichi visited, I took the opportunity to accept coffee and lunch invitations with friends. They were flexible with time and understood the need for last-minute changes, which happened on a few occasions. We met in coffee shops and restaurants, all within a ten-minute walk of the hospital. Though my antennas were up for a phone call from the hospital, I enjoyed the chats to give an update on Deirdre, but also to hear about my friends' lives. I found that the buoyant atmosphere of animated conversations, and the smells of cooked fish, meats, and baked goods were a refreshing change from the hospital.

Every night, I expected a phone call from Deirdre, but none came. Daichi arrived at a perfect time for both of us. He filled Deirdre with joy by his presence at her side and gave me much-needed respite. I slept well most nights.

Every evening, Daichi came to my house for dinner and a shower. He was usually at the house for about two hours, and during that time I would drive down and stay with Deirdre. He had a generous amount of hair and Deirdre warned me he would be in the bathroom for quite a while.

"The Japanese guys spend a lot of time grooming their hair," she said with an impish grin.

She felt too sick for visitors. Conor worked evenings and Aisling had to study. One evening, I made a chicken and broccoli casserole, topped with mozzarella cheese and baked breadcrumbs, and took it to Deirdre's room. Another time I baked salmon, potatoes, and green beans, which Deirdre liked. I put dishes, cutlery, napkins, and the meal into one large nylon bag and managed to get everything to Deirdre's room intact.

Aisling visited at suppertime so we could eat together. Deirdre enjoyed this time. She ate small portions and I put the leftovers in the fridge for Daichi to eat later. He appreciated everything I cooked; after he ate and his plate was clean, he thanked me profusely.

Daichi's devotion to Deirdre was unwavering. He spent the entire ten-day visit in the hospital with her. Two or three times I encouraged him to take a walk down Spring Garden Road. He went to Starbucks and studied for a course that he was taking in college. On the first day, after he returned to Deirdre's room, he looked a little shaken.

"I am very happy to be back here in Deirdre's room," he said, standing in front of the window. "Some of those people out there are scary."

He had come across street people who were persistent in trying to get money from him. This was something new for Daichi, but I assured him they were harmless, despite their appearance and begging habits. After he got used to them, he relaxed and laughed when Deirdre and I teased him about his initial reaction.

On Wednesday, April 23, day thirteen of chemo, Deirdre had another bone marrow biopsy—part of the normal protocol. Daichi opted to stay and hold Deirdre's hand during the procedure. I had explained the procedure to him beforehand, and tried to paint a clear picture of what it was like. I sat close to him, ready to pick him off the floor if he fainted. He sat on a chair facing Deirdre and held her hand while she lay on her side. Donna, Nebojsa, and the resident talked to us and asked Daichi questions about himself.

Daichi was nervous at first, averting his eyes from the activities behind Deirdre's back. He distracted himself by talking to her. When Nebojsa produced the large bore needle and began to twist it into Deirdre's hip bone, Daichi's face turned pale. His whole body tensed. He looked paralysed with fear for Deirdre, and watching him made me anxious. For five minutes an intense silence filled the room, punctuated by Nebojsa's voice when he asked Deirdre about pain. I gently suggested to Daichi that I could sit with Deirdre.

"Oh no. I'm good," he protested in a broken voice as he rubbed his forehead with his free hand. When the procedure was completed, he walked swiftly out the door.

"That was so terrifying," he said when he came back a few moments later, his face still pale. "The way he dug that big needle into your hip—"

"You shouldn't have looked at that needle," Deirdre said, waving her hand and looking at him from her lying position, a big grin on her face. She had one other biopsy during Daichi's visit; he left the room while it was being done.

One day Deirdre asked me if I could find her a board game. Aisling and I looked around the stores and finally found one called Sorry!. Deirdre was to become fixated on the game and would challenge Daichi to a game whenever she felt well enough. Sometimes before I walked in the room, I could hear them laughing together, conveying their immense joy to those outside the room—an uplifting display of two people in love.

On April 23, Wednesday, Deirdre's neck and shoulders ached. The sinus pain was worse and she vomited frequently. The nurses stopped weaning the morphine drip. For most of the day, Deirdre sat upright in bed, holding a cold facecloth against the left side of her face. A blue heating pad lay wrapped around her neck and shoulders.

A chest X-ray taken the day before showed a fungal infection in one lung—a common complication among people with acute leukemia. Later that afternoon, the resident came into the room and told Deirdre she was going to start a potent antifungal IV drug, amphotericin B. Deirdre was already taking an antifungal pill, fluconazole—considered a pea-shooter in strength compared to the cannonball effects the amphotericin B would deliver.

The resident said she was reluctant to give this drug because of its toxic side effects, such as kidney and liver damage, but the infection needed aggressive treatment. After she left the room I tried to reassure Deirdre by telling her that her organs were young and that she'd do fine.

"It can't be much worse than this," she said, leaning forward, her head down, her hand pressed against the side of her face. The fever had seesawed since her arrival, but now it remained consistently high. She was taking Tylenol and codeine every four hours, along with the morphine drip.

That afternoon the nurse gave the first dose of IV amphotericin B through a port in the hickman line. On Friday morning the blood reports showed that the kidneys, liver, and other organs were healthy and working well. During the previous few days, she'd had daily platelet transfusions. Today they were borderline low and the doctors felt she could forego a transfusion. The effects of the chemo drugs were now at their peak and they had obliterated most of the bad, but also the good cells, leaving Deirdre wide open to any kind of bug attack.

By Friday evening her face was puffy, about twice its normal size, and there were numerous petechiae—pinpoint red spots—speckled all over it. She had a burning fever; her hair was damp with sweat around the hairline and the sinus pain, she said, was excruciating. Her whole body was swollen and dotted with petechiae. Tears continued to fall along the sides of the cloth that she held against her face. Daichi sat on the bed beside her, holding her in his arms.

Despite Deirdre's misery, she was still considerate of Daichi.

"You're here at my worst time," she said, holding the facecloth away from her face and looking at him apologetically.

"Well, Deirdre," he said, considering a moment longer, "it's good that I'm here at your worst time and I'm happy I can help you at your worst time."

I kept myself busy, refreshing the facecloth with ice-cold water, turning her pillow over, reheating the neck pad in the microwave and trying to anticipate her needs. Meanwhile, my heart was doing its pronounced thumping as I tried to project an air of calmness. Once in a while, I perched on the edge of a chair and offered words of comfort.

Nebojsa dropped in around 6:00 PM, before he left for the weekend. He said her symptoms could be due to the side effects of the amphotericin B, the aftermath of the chemo drugs, the fungal infection, or for other reasons; it was impossible to isolate the cause. After he assessed her, he decided that she needed a platelet transfusion, which the nurse gave an hour or so later.

Deirdre was happy that Aisling was away.

I'm glad Aisling isn't here for this," she said. "She would have been so upset." I was also relieved that Aisling was not there to see Deirdre in this state of misery.

Around 1:00 AM, Deirdre had been asleep for half an hour and Daichi encouraged me to go home to get some sleep. He assured me that he would call if I was needed. I reluctantly left for home.

As I lay awake in bed my mind kept churning, imagining all the catastrophic outcomes that could befall Deirdre: hemorrhage, septic shock, total organ failure. She could stop breathing—

Please God, let her get better.

When I called the nurse around 4 AM, she said that Deirdre was a little better. She and Daichi were sleeping the last time she'd looked in the room. I felt a little relieved, but I still couldn't sleep. I had to see for myself.

At 7:00 AM, when I got back to the room, they were both asleep. A few minutes later, when Deirdre opened her eyes to look at me, I asked about the pain.

"It's much better," she said, her voice barely audible. "I hope it stays away."

When she sat up against the pillows, I noticed the swelling in her face was significantly reduced and the petechiae spots had decreased considerably.

I felt relieved, like I'd woken up from a bad dream. I sat on a chair and let my body relax.

Daichi woke up and half-opened his eyes. He looked like he hadn't slept in days. After he and Deirdre exchanged a few mumbled words, they went back to sleep. Confident that the worst was over, I went back home again, snuggled under my down-filled duvet, and sank into a deep sleep.

Chapter 12

END OF CHEMOTHERAPY

No matter what is thrown at me, I will get right back up. It is
what we are here for and what we all go through. So I can stop
carrying things with me and letting them all stick. I can get up and
go through, live it and survive it. I can do things right, make good
decisions, and help others to find strength. —Deirdre's diary, 2002

It was Sunday, April 27, and Deirdre had gone from moribund just two days
before to cheerful and talkative. Though her face was pale and drawn, her eyes
dull, and her hair frizzed, she had a serenity about her, like she'd survived a
hurricane at sea and landed on a warm beach.

The pain had subsided, the swelling had disappeared, and her tiny frame
was displayed again. She ate half a bowl of bran mixture for breakfast and
by midday had challenged Daichi to two games of Sorry!. That morning,
the blood counts increased for the first time, signalling the end of the chemo
attack. A bone marrow biopsy, planned for the following day, would tell if
the myeloid leukemia was in remission. The nurses were pulling back on the
morphine drip again.

For this round of chemo, the worst was over. As the sunlight gleamed
through the window, it lifted my spirits further. I sat there, full of delight
and gratitude.

On Monday, five of Deirdre's friends came to visit. They stayed for twenty
minutes. After she introduced them to Daichi, one of them asked her how
she was.

"Oh man, I had such a gross week, I don't want to talk about it," she said,
flicking a hand in the direction of the five sombre faces. "So, what's going on
out there?"

Ten minutes later, the room was filled with laugher as her friends competed to tell funny anecdotes of times past and present. Deirdre's laughter tumbled out above it all. It was uplifting to listen to those young people, and to hear the faith and optimism they held for the future.

Deirdre talked about going back to Japan. Later, in her own time, she would recognize the adversities and difficulties of this dream; her medical condition would prevent her from ever returning to Japan. Take things one day at a time.

Daichi blended in with her friends and participated in the animated conversation. Before the five left, they planned to go out together when Daichi returned in September. Deirdre reminded them that she would be going home on the weekend. That magical word "home" was now being tossed about. Sometimes I found it daunting as I imagined an array of potential mishaps. What if she caught a bad infection? The white blood counts were still well below normal. The platelets were still way down—she could bleed to death in the middle of the night. What if that awful pain came back? I felt like a new mother bringing her newborn baby home. 8B had become a safe haven, a bubble—it provided protection from the forces outside. Whenever these nightmarish thoughts plagued me, I meditated until I became calm and positive again.

Deirdre, unaware of my wild imaginings, was excited to be going home. Her blood counts were low, but stable enough that she could leave the hospital in a few days. They would continue to climb over the next ten days before it was time to return and have the lymphoblastic leukemia treatment.

Aisling arrived home that evening after spending a wonderful weekend in California. She had called once or twice a day while she was away. When I talked to her on the phone I didn't tell her how miserable Deirdre had been, seeing no sense in harrowing her with disheartening news.

She came into the room and I saw the delight in her face when she recognized a trace of the old, vibrant Deirdre.

"You look so much livelier, Deirdre," she said.

"You wouldn't believe how bad I was," Deirdre said. "On Friday night, I thought I was going to die. You were lucky you weren't here." She continued to recount some of her sufferings.

"Oh, Deirdre, I can't believe the hell you've been through," Aisling said, eyes wide and moist, as she put her arms around Deirdre's shoulders. "It must have been horrible."

"Oh, well. Thank God it's over with now," Deirdre said with a prolonged sigh of relief.

The resident discontinued the amphotericin B after Monday's X-ray, and restarted Deirdre back the fluconazole, which she would continue at home.

The fungal infection, although not completely cleared, was much smaller. The nausea and sweating continued to wax and wane as the morphine withdrawals persisted.

She began to eat more. Friends brought in homemade biscuits, vegetarian lasagna, fruit trays, and soup. She craved her favourite Dairy Queen sundae. She would have a look of utter satisfaction on her face as she spooned it into her mouth, wallowing in the taste of the strawberries and chocolate sauce that floated over the soft ice cream.

If they weren't playing Sorry!, she and Daichi watched DVD movies or read. Her friends brought in books: *The Memory Keeper's Daughter, Blankets*... Some had funny stories with cartoon pictures. Sometimes Daichi would sit beside her on the bed, showing her funny passages from these manga novels he read. They sat shoulder to shoulder and shared the funny parts. Right on cue, they'd turn their heads, look at each other, and then let out a bout of loud jovial laughter. Nebojsa referred to them as "a cute couple."

Later, on Monday evening, I went to Mollie's house for supper. She had made a Caesar salad and a beer can chicken cooked in the barbeque. Her homemade apple pie with ice cream on top tasted delicious. We washed the meal down with a glass of red wine and chatted until I left at 8:00 PM.

I walked home under dark purple clouds that filled the sky. The wind whipped the bare branches. Sprinkles of rain fell on my face, making me feel more alive. I was thankful, optimistic that our lives would eventually get back on course.

On Tuesday, in preparation for discharge, the staff encouraged Deirdre to go outside the unit, but she was reluctant to leave the sanctuary of her room, afraid she'd catch a germ. After we persuaded her to venture out of the unit, I found a wheelchair and Daichi and I rolled her down the corridor, past walls with paintings and plaques donated by former patients' families. We went as far as the elevators.

I remembered when Deirdre was first admitted, how I'd read an engraving on one of those plaques—it had been donated by the family of a twenty-year-old who had passed on. A sudden feeling of dread filled me. *What if Deirdre passed on?* After that, I looked straight ahead whenever I walked through there.

Deirdre was happy to be outside, but after ten minutes she wanted to go back to bed. She was still frail and fragile, her neck and shoulders began to hurt, and the nausea started again. When she lay back in her bed, the nurse gave her Gravol and codeine. I massaged her shoulders and neck and after half an hour, she felt hungry and sat up, ready for something to eat.

She had the biopsy procedure that afternoon which Aisling came and stayed for. Daichi and Conor took the elevators and went to the cafeteria. Deirdre liked it when both Aisling and I were present during procedures. Aisling kept the air light and the jokes going, while I listened for information from the staff and the asked questions.

The procedure went smoothly. I never overcame that urge to cringe when Nebojsa twisted the big needle into Deirdre's hip bone. "It's almost done," I would say to Deirdre, as much to comfort myself as her.

Daichi was to leave the next day, Wednesday. He would return in September—after Deirdre received the bone marrow transplant. Worried about her reaction to Daichi's departure, I reminded her to look forward to September. She nodded her head in agreement—to keep me happy, I'm sure.

On the evening before he left, Daichi had his shower at the hospital, in a bathroom down the corridor by the elevators. I brought supper to Deirdre's room and then left to allow them time alone together. Daichi's flight was at 9:00 AM.

Aisling and I planned to meet in Deirdre's room at 7:00 AM and she would stay with Deirdre while I took Daichi to the airport.

The next morning I was awake at 5:30. I worried that Daichi's flight might not leave on time. I had experienced many flight delays over the years, especially when I worked in the Arctic. Daichi was to attend an important family reunion in southern Japan, a six-hour drive from Tokyo, the day after his return. If he missed today's flight, it meant missing the reunion.

I turned the computer on and looked up the departures from the Halifax airport. His flight, Continental Airlines to Newark, showed on the screen. Cancelled.

It was 6:30 before I could talk to anyone at Continental. They had already changed Daichi's flight to the following day. The other airlines were full today.

At 7:00 AM, I called Daichi and told him about the cancellation. I asked him to call Aisling; I would try to book him on a different flight out today.

Six phone calls and two hours later, Air Canada booked him on a flight to Toronto. It would connect with the flight to Tokyo that afternoon.

The flight was leaving at 10:00 AM. It was now 8:45 and the drive to the airport would take half an hour. I called Daichi and told him I would pick him up outside the hospital in ten minutes. He would call Aisling. I had no idea if we would make it on time; I had assured Air Canada that we would.

After I picked up Daichi and drove to the airport—I managed to drive reasonably close to the speed limit—we got to the checkout counter. Five more minutes and it would have been closed. Daichi's flight was leaving in half an hour.

On the way to the airport Daichi thanked me, and said how much he liked Halifax.

"When Deirdre was in Japan, I never knew she had this many friends here—that there are so many people who care so much about her," he said. "I'm very happy that she made it home and that she is with you guys." He talked about how much he loved Deirdre. I thanked him for coming and for helping to build Deirdre up after the illness and drugs had brought her to her knees.

We hugged one another before he went through security. When he looked back and waved, we both had a few tears trickling down our cheeks.

After I arrived home and parked the car in the driveway, I walked straight to the hospital. When I got to her room, Deirdre was sitting on the big armchair by the side of the window, clattering on her laptop. She looked relaxed. Aisling sat on another chair beside her, reading.

"He was happy when you called and told him about the flight being cancelled," she said with a grin. "He would have liked another day here." She said that Daichi's sudden departure, having to run out of her room at the last minute, was a good thing because it left them little time for prolonged good-byes.

"It was easier to say good-bye when we had to do it so fast," she added.

I was relieved to see Deirdre reasonably content. We were both happy that Daichi would make it home for the reunion.

That afternoon the results of the biopsy came back. The myeloid leukemia was in remission. We were ecstatic. The blood counts continued to climb. The hourly rate on the morphine drip was down to 4 cc an hour and it could soon be discontinued.

Ann and Deirdre—April 2008

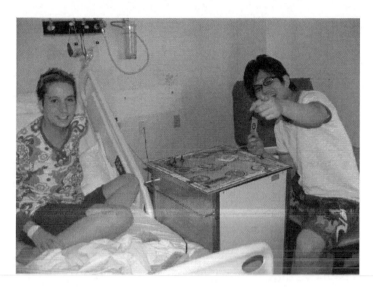

Deirdre and Daichi—April 2008

Chapter 13

Hair Loss

The discovery of self is a difficult thing and possibly there are those who never venture on this journey. Who knew how great life is when you give yourself more experiences? —Deirdre's diary, 2002

After the chemo treatment was underway, the nurses advised Deirdre to have her hair cut in stages. It would lessen the shock of sudden total hair loss. Her friend Orla, a hairdresser, came to her room to cut it. Deirdre, Aisling, and Orla had taken Irish dance lessons together as children.

Aisling and I pushed the chairs and bedside table off to the side, giving Orla more working space. In preparation, Orla slipped the loop of her hairdresser's apron over her head, tied the strings at her back, covered Deirdre's shoulders with a nylon wrap, and wet her hair. She rummaged through a black bag, pulling out a scissors, shears, hairbrush, and hairdryer, and put them on the bedside table.

Aisling and I stayed and chatted. Deirdre sat upright on the bed. Her back rested against the pillows, her head leaned forward. Her face was relaxed, her eyes half closed, and she joined in the conversation now and then.

Orla manoeuvred her nimble fingers like a surgeon. Picking up a small bunch of hair between two fingers of one hand, she used the sharp scissors with her other hand. She cut straight across the strands of hair before they fell from her fingers, leaving clear, sharp edges. When she finished, Deirdre had a chic-looking hairstyle.

On Thursday, for the third morning in a row, wisps of hair were scattered over Deirdre's pillow. Deirdre stood by the bed and surveyed the pillow, a pensive look on her face.

"I think it's time for the head shave," she said calmly, as though it was time to have her fingernails clipped.

"It would be better to have it done before you go home," I said. "Are you okay with it?"

"Oh yeah," she answered. "I don't want it falling out all over the place after I leave here."

I asked one of the nurses how I would go about shaving Deirdre's head. They had a special razor in the unit and I was very relieved when the nurse offered to do the shaving.

Deirdre sat on a chair, a towel around her shoulders. Her eyes were wide. With a half-smile on her face, she looked up at me standing beside her.

"I wonder what I'll look like?" she asked.

"*Mmm.* Sinead O'Connor." I laughed.

"Too bad I just spent two hundred dollars on my hair," she said, smiling ruefully. She'd had it highlighted and styled in Japan before coming home.

While the nurse distracted Deirdre, asking her questions about herself, she gently rotated the razor back and forth across her scalp until it was bare and smooth. Deirdre thanked her, got up and walked to the bathroom. She looked in the mirror and put her hands over the sides of her face. As her eyes widened, she began to laugh.

"Oh my God! I look so weird," she shrieked. "But I'm sure I'll get used to this new style. Wait 'til Aisling sees this." She shook her head slowly and laughed again.

A little later, Nebojsa came through the door. He stopped dead in his tracks when he saw Deirdre's new hairstyle.

"Wow," he said, "you look so much younger." He turned and pointed to a picture of Deirdre and Daichi on the wall, her hair shoulder-length and blond. "This is—well, okay—but..." He turned back to her. "But this looks so much better," he said emphatically.

"Thank you," Deirdre said, laughing exuberantly, putting her hands on her head.

Two weeks later, at home, when wisps of hair sprouted on her head, I said that maybe we shaved it too soon.

"Oh well, I may as well have the full experience," she said, as if she had chosen to partake in some radical culture.

On Thursday, May 1, Deirdre walked around her room trying to get the strength back into her legs. Her steps were slow and protracted, as if she were walking on ice. Sometimes, watching her, I forgot how lively she used to be, when she would choose to walk everywhere rather than take a bus or drive. Dancing was her passion then.

At five years of age, she had begun taking Irish dance lessons—now known as the "River Dance" style. She eventually became a champion dancer with a graceful, fluid style of her own. When she listened to a "jig tune" she could leap high in the air like a deer. When she danced to the music of a reel, she could weave an intricate dance pattern across the floor on tiptoe, moving with the speed of a hummingbird.

To do a "hard shoe" dance, she wore shoes with two-inch-high, square heels and a strap that tied across the top. A piece of fibreglass was glued to the heel and toe of the soles. When she danced she would pound the floor with the soles of the shoes, switching from heel to toe in rapid succession. She would swivel her feet around as though they were attached to her ankle joints by elastic bands. The fibreglass tips created a drumming sound. When Deirdre danced in perfect time to the musical accompaniment, she blended the rhythm of the drumming sound in with the rhythm of the music, creating perfect harmony between the two.

On Thursday morning, Nebojsa gave us an update. Deirdre could go home the following day if the morning blood counts were up. The morphine drip was down to 3 cc an hour. It could be shut off tomorrow and she could also come off the IV antibiotic. Nebojsa said an appointment would be made for her to return as an outpatient the following Friday for a bone marrow biopsy. They needed to see what the lymphoblastic leukemia and her cells were doing.

We kept our fingers crossed.

Conor and I wheeled her down to the cafeteria during lunch. She rarely ate from the hospital food tray anymore. Today she ate half a bowl of chicken noodle soup and a biscuit from Tim Hortons. We sat for fifteen minutes by the wall-to-wall windows in the cafeteria while the sun beamed in at us. Deirdre looked out, a smile on her face.

"I can't wait to get out there," she said. "Maybe we can go to the beach some day?"

"Maybe we'll drive out there next week if you're feeling up to it," I answered, hoping she'd change her mind by then; she could get a chill out there.

That afternoon I drove back to the house to prepare for Deirdre's homecoming. Before I left, I gathered up most of her belongings and took them with me. When I got home I changed into my old blue jeans and sweatshirt, put on rubber gloves, and prepared to swoop through the house on a cleaning frenzy. I cleaned the kitchen sink, the two bathroom sinks, the counter tops, toilets, and bathtub, and I vacuumed all the floors. From the cabinet under the sink, I got a floor bucket and rag. I half-filled the bucket with lukewarm water and liquid soap, went on my hands and knees, and washed the pine kitchen floor, the hardwood floors on the first level, and the tiled bathroom floors.

I damp-dusted in Deirdre's bedroom. It was situated in the middle of the upstairs next to my room. It had a double bed made of dark pine, a night table with a lamp on top, a dresser, and a mirror. A salt crystal lamp sat on the floor by a wall. A window above the bed, covered with a venetian blind and purple sheer curtains, looked onto the driveway and the neighbours' backyards. Pictures with different scenes, one done in needlepoint, hung on the cream-coloured walls.

A few days before, I had told the contractors about Deirdre's homecoming. They completed all the work that afternoon. The door was painted the same orangey-red colour that Deirdre had chosen a few years before.

That evening, concerned about Deirdre's comfort and considering her weakened immune system, I went to Costco with our friends Valerie and Paul and bought a new mattress for her bed. The mattress fit in their van and in less than an hour, we were back home again. Paul helped me put the old mattress out on the curb for garbage pickup. He also gave us four Styrofoam containers full of frozen hamburger soup and pea soup that he had made. The hamburger soup was chock full of vegetables: red peppers, peas, carrots, tomatoes, and onions. The pea soup had split peas, carrots, onions, celery, and chicken broth.

Aisling and I put the new mattress on the bed frame and made the bed up with new sheets and a sandy-coloured, down duvet. We went to the Bay department store and bought underwear and socks for Deirdre. Daichi had mailed her belongings from Japan but they still hadn't arrived.

Aisling gave Deirdre some of her clothes—they had similar tastes. Before she went to Japan, Aisling had relied on Deirdre to help her choose which clothes to buy.

I took all the clothes home and laundered them.

On Thursday and Friday, Deirdre occupied herself by reading some of Daichi's letters. He had sent one every day before his visit. They e-mailed back and forth at least twice a day since he returned to Japan. Deirdre said that he gave her updates on the family reunion. Numerous relatives from around Japan had come and she said he was happy to have made it there.

After getting her arts degree, Deirdre had taken a one-year course in public relations at Nova Scotia Community College in Halifax. The students in her class decided they would make supper for her every evening after she came home from hospital. They got together and planned which days each one would cook and deliver the food.

Throughout Deirdre's illness, I was frequently amazed and heartened that a situation this horrific could extract the beautiful essence that resides in the core of everybody: kindness, compassion, and love, like the bright stars that shine through the sky in the darkest, coldest nights.

Friday morning, Dr. White came on rounds. It was official; she could go home that day. The blood counts were up. He would see Deirdre in ten days, and let her know the next plan of treatment. He told her to rest, go outside, and eat well to build up her stamina before the next round of chemo.

The nurse discontinued the morphine drip and the IV antibiotic. She plugged the lumen ports of the hickman line with a sterile rubber stopper and injected saline water through them to keep the lumens patent. The hickman line would remain until after the transplant, longer if needed. The nurse gave Deirdre a special pin, and showed her how to tie the lumens onto her shirt to prevent accidental removal.

Deirdre, sporting a floral bandana on her head, wore a pink nightgown over blue capris. I took a picture of her to send to Daichi. They had a nickname for the IV fluid—José. I never found out where the name came from.

She e-mailed him the picture and wrote, "Look, no José."

The resident gave us a prescription for oral antibiotics, antifungal pills, and Tylenol 3. The nurse handed us a yellow, laminated plastic card to put on the fridge at home. It listed signs and symptoms to watch for: cough, fever, bleeding, etc. If Deirdre showed signs of any of these, we were to call the hospital. Nebojsa told her to go outside and get plenty of fresh air.

It was about 3:00 PM when we went to the nurses' desk and said good-bye to everyone. Anyone who worked that day came to see Deirdre off. She sat in the wheelchair and Aisling and I rolled her down to the main door of the hospital.

Conor was waiting outside with the car. As she walked from the wheelchair to the car, I put my arm around her achingly small waist, scared she'd faint and fall on the pavement.

While we drove home, Deirdre—with a serene look on her face—looked out the window, turning her head from side to side. The trees were starting to leaf, and the sun, slipping in and out between fluffy white clouds, brought crowds of people out walking. Some wore shorts and T-shirts. It was the month of May, the month of renewal.

Aisling and Deirdre, ready to dance—May 2002

Chapter 14
HOME FROM THE HOSPITAL: THE ADJUSTMENT

I see how much pain there is involved in truly living. Pain is something every true living person experiences. It is what we need to bring us together. It doesn't kill us but helps us to grow. True sorrow is something vital, but blinded sorrow poisons. Some just can't see that and let it drive them crazy. —Deirdre's diary, 2001

We arrived home from the hospital around 3:30 PM. Deirdre winced a little as she stepped from the car. Then she walked slowly up the seven steps to the front door.

"I'm glad you kept that colour," she said, looking at the door. "The place looks really good."

When we got inside, she took her light green coat and boots off. She wore a dark rose-coloured dress over black Lycra tights and a cotton cardigan. She walked straight into the living room, just to the left past the front door. Exhausted from the short journey home, she lay down on the couch.

Aisling went upstairs and got a pillow while I draped a blanket over Deirdre. Symptoms of the morphine withdrawal started to rear their ugly heads again. She said she felt nauseated and slightly achy all over. The sweating started. I took her temperature and it was normal. I gave her a Gravol pill and two Tylenol pills that I took from the kitchen cupboard, and then turned on the gas fireplace. After ten minutes, she closed her eyes and fell asleep. Aisling and Conor left—Aisling, for class; Conor, for work.

Half an hour later, she woke up, said she felt better and asked for something to drink. I went and got her a glass of club soda from the fridge—a family remedy for most stomach ailments.

Twenty years ago, on a visit to Ireland, Deirdre contracted a stomach flu.

She was five years old at the time. After five days of vomiting and subsequent dehydration, the local doctor advised me to take her to the hospital for IV fluid. My eighty-year-old aunt came to look after Aisling and Conor, and after she arrived in the house she said, "Give her a few mouthfuls of soda water. That'll settle her stomach." After we found some, Deirdre drank a glassful of the soda water and kept it down. I cancelled the hospital visit.

Today, she drank a glassful and kept it down.

"I'd like to go upstairs," she said after a while, pushing the blanket away as if it weighed a ton.

I was one step behind her as she walked gingerly up the stairs, holding onto the rail, exaggerating the lift of her steps, afraid of tripping. When she got to the top, she stopped for a few minutes to catch her breath and then walked into the small room at the end of the narrow hallway. The room had a love seat that stood in front of a window looking onto the street. Green curtains draped the sides of the window, framed photographs and two Inuit tapestries decorated the yellow walls. The TV sat on a wooden table with books and magazines underneath.

Deirdre picked up a magazine, walked into her bedroom, and lay in bed. She said she felt nauseated again, and asked for a two-litre ice cream container that she would use to vomit into. By the time I ran downstairs and returned with the container, the nausea had passed. She was sitting up in the bed looking at an old knitted, stuffed doll that she'd had as a child. It wore a blue dress with a red bonnet and one eye was missing.

"I always liked this doll," she said, straightening the dress with her hands, a pensive look on her face. "She looks scary with that missing eye."

"If it scares you that much, Deirdre," I joked, "I guess I'll just have to do an eye transplant and use a needle and thread as a donor."

She picked up the *Us Weekly* magazine and leafed through it. I allowed her some time to be alone and went downstairs to putter around for a little while. When I went back up, she was leaning forward on the bed, hands over her face, crying. I sat and put my arms around her.

"What's the matter, Deirdre?" I asked, sensing a melancholy about her.

"I don't know, all of a sudden I feel really lonely and sad," she whimpered.

"It's normal to feel like this, Deirdre," I said. "Coming home is another adjustment with everything else that's gone on in your life. I remember that time when you broke your arm, and the first day you came home from the hospital you cried a bit. Then you were okay. This is a much bigger thing, but you'll soon get over it."

When she was nine years old, she had sustained a compound fracture to her arm after falling from a slide. She was in Cape Breton, a four-hour ambulance ride from Halifax. She spent three days in hospital afterwards.

After we talked for a while, she cheered up a little. We went downstairs and I walked one step ahead of her. For the first three days after she returned home, I continued to guard her as though she were a toddler whenever she walked up and down the stairs. When we got to the kitchen, she sat by the counter and ate half a bowl of pea soup and a morsel of homemade brown soda bread that our friends Gill and Bob had dropped off—the soda bread was Bob's specialty.

At 6:30 PM, her friends Tom and Graeme came to visit. Tom had baked a dozen vanilla cupcakes with pink-coloured icing on top. Afraid she might aggravate the nausea, Deirdre saved hers for the next day; she sipped on tea and club soda instead. The rest of us had tea and one of the cupcakes, which tasted sweet and delicious.

While they visited, I took the opportunity to go to Shoppers Drug Mart and pick up Tylenol 3, the antibiotic, and the antifungal drug prescriptions that were ready. When I came back, they were sitting around the coffee table in the living room. The board game Sorry! was spread over the glass coffee table. They were in the midst of the game and Deirdre's face was fixed on the board. She looked like she was concentrating on the next strategy. "This is the only thing I have any attention span for right now," she said.

At 9:30, after everybody left, she went to bed, flipped open her laptop, and sent an e-mail to Daichi. Twenty minutes later, she lay down and drifted to sleep.

Her bedroom was dimly lit by the salt crystal light. I kept her door and my bedroom door wide open. I dozed off and on, waking up frequently, cocking my ear to listen to her breathing.

At 3:00 AM, when I heard Deirdre's bed frame creak a little, I got up and went into her room. Her shoulders, neck, and head ached, and the nausea was back. I gave her two Tylenol 3s and a Gravol. After I took her temperature—which was normal—she swallowed the pills with water and lay down beside me in my bed, feeling sad and lonely again. After we talked awhile, and I told her to think ahead to four months from now when the treatments and transplant would over, she went back to sleep. I was still awake when the dawn's early light came through the window, thankful that Deirdre's first night home was over and uneventful.

Deirdre's crying spells continued for four days. My heart ached for her. I was running out of comforting words. Whenever she was on her own for more than five minutes, reading or watching TV, a fresh waterfall of tears would erupt. Talking to Daichi twice a day on Skype gave her some solace.

"I'm scared," she said. "I feel like there's something heavy and dark pulling me down inside."

I had expected she would feel some sadness after she got home, but after watching her go through this pain and anguish for three days at this intensity, I became very disconcerted. At the end of the third day, she agreed to have a reiki treatment from my friend Barbara.

When Barbara came, Deirdre lay on the couch, fully dressed, with a blanket over her. Barbara placed her hands over different areas of Deirdre's body, barely touching her as she held them over each area for about five minutes. Deirdre began to relax. She closed her eyes, looking like she was sleeping. Half an hour later, Barbara gently withdrew her hands from Deirdre's feet, signalling the end of the treatment. Deirdre, her eyes half-open, smiled up at Barbara and said, "Thank you Barbara, I feel nice and relaxed now."

She slept for five hours straight that night.

Until Deirdre came home from the hospital, she'd had no time to think about the bombshell that had hit her, the immensity of its devastation, the uprooting that destroyed every facet of her life as she knew it. The physical pain and discomfort, the journey home from Japan, the tests, the procedures, the chemo, the emotional swings of bad news and good news, and the overall hustle and bustle of hospital life, all served to block any thoughts of the harsher reality. Now, at home, devoid of noise and distraction, the sword of clarity had time to pierce through to her mind: her shattered dreams, her uncertain future, her restricted lifestyle—like a bird that just had its wings clipped. One day I held her in my arms as tears streaked down her face. She sobbed uncontrollably and looked particularly dejected.

"I miss Daichi. I miss my life in Japan and I don't know when I'll be able to go back," she cried, "I can't do anything for myself. I hate being like this. I don't even have my clothes and all my other stuff."

She brightened up when friends came, but the sadness lurked behind the weak smile, ready to erupt like a volcano at any moment. Aisling was extremely concerned about Deirdre and visited every day. She stayed as long as her studies allowed her.

Because of the persistent nausea, pain, sweating spells, and sadness, Deirdre saw few people during those first four days. To keep her mind occupied, we sat in the room and watched reruns of *The Office* on DVD. Before that, I had rarely taken the time to watch DVDs and my television usually remained unplugged. I began to enjoy the shows and found this time with Deirdre very relaxing. We laughed together at some of the funny cynical comments. Not having to go anywhere or do anything was a nice change for me.

During the first few days at home, after covering the lumens of the hickman line with small plastic bags, I helped Deirdre in and out of the bathtub. By the third day she managed on her own.

"You must feel like you have a baby to look after again," she said when I offered to help her. "I want to do this myself."

"Right now I wouldn't want to be doing anything else, Deirdre," I answered, sensing her vulnerability and sensitivity. "But I agree. It would be good for your mental health to bathe yourself."

On Monday, May 4, a beautiful sunny spring day, Aisling called and suggested we take Deirdre to Lawrencetown Beach, half an hour's drive away. I was reluctant at first, but when Deirdre's eyes lit up and she nodded her head enthusiastically, I agreed. She dressed warmly: two sweaters under her light green cotton coat, tights, pants and boots, her pink striped bandana, and a cotton scarf around her neck. I wore a fleece jacket over a sweater and jeans. Aisling came and picked us up in her blue Protégé. Deirdre sat in the front seat and I sat in the back, holding onto the two-litre ice cream container—just in case.

Apart from short waves of nausea, she tolerated the drive well.

When we arrived at the beach, we parked beside the entrance to the boardwalk. The day was crisp and warm at 20°C and there was very little wind. We went onto the boardwalk and slowly walked the short distance to the other end.

"This feels so awesome," Deirdre said, looking at the sun illuminating the white-rimmed waves that folded and unfolded over the moist sand. The sky above was a pale blue. Blankets of white fluffy clouds glided slowly and gracefully above the horizon. We stood at the end of the boardwalk for ten minutes and took some pictures; though I didn't show it, I fretted about Deirdre catching a cold. After we got back in the car, we headed back toward the city.

"That was so refreshing," Deirdre said, looking out the window at the dense clusters of spruce trees, the low marshland, and houses sparsely sprinkled on either side.

We passed by Rainbow Haven Beach. When Deirdre, Conor, and Aisling were children, we would go there a few times a week during the summer months. We would arrive at 10:00 AM and leave when the wind came up around 2:30 PM. Very often, my friend Rosemary Gribbin and her children joined us.

Rosemary and I would sit on a beach blanket and watch the children play in the sand. They'd jump into the salt water now and then to cool off. We brought thermoses full of tea that we poured into mugs and sipped on while we were there. We had picnic baskets with egg and lettuce sandwiches, peanut butter and jam sandwiches, homemade cookies, and apples. Deirdre had never eaten an egg in her life; eggs and cucumbers "made her gag."

On July 15, 1982, I had been sitting on the beach in Rainbow Haven, heavily pregnant with Deirdre. Later that afternoon, I began to feel the twinges of labour pains. After an hour of intermittent contractions, I left and went to the maternity hospital in Halifax. At 9:17 PM, Deirdre glided smoothly and fluidly into the world.

Today, as we drove along, she asked, "Maybe we can come back here another day?" I agreed to return with her.

Aisling, Deirdre, Tom, and Graeme playing Sorry!—May 2008

Aisling and Deirdre visiting the beach—May 2008

Chapter *15*

Days at Home

I will rid myself of the assumption that every waking moment
is happiness. Without sadness, I would be no one, just a
goof, and a stupid one at that.—Deirdre's diary, 2002

By Wednesday, May 7, the sadness that besieged Deirdre had dissipated. Her stamina had increased and a little of her old spunky self began to shine through. The nausea, achiness, and sweating had finally subsided. Every morning, she made her bed and tidied her room before going downstairs for breakfast. She and Daichi talked twice a day on Skype, using a webcam to see one another. After their conversation ended, around 9:30 PM, she would walk to the bathroom, brush her teeth, and shout goodnight. I would drop into her room before she turned on her iPod and lay down to sleep.

After I plugged the salt crystal lamp into the wall socket, I closed her bedroom door and got into my own bed. I read for a while and gave thanks that we had made it this far. Confident that she'd survive the night without my perpetual vigilance, I no longer fretted when her bedroom door was closed—when all I could see of her room was the dull orange glow of light spilling through the crack in the door. Now that her steps were so much stronger, I also cut the imaginary umbilical cord that tied us together when she walked up and down the stairs.

On a few occasions, despite a surplus of food in the kitchen, she pulled saucepans and cooking utensils from the cupboards and made spaghetti or chili.

"I want to feel like I'm normal again," she would say as she continued to cook. She listened to *Vampire Weekend* and other CDs as she poured beans, canned tomatoes, and spices into a pot. She chopped up red peppers, green peppers, celery, onions, and mushrooms to add to the mixture. Some days she walked out into the backyard and looked at the flower bed. The orange lilies that had made their way well past the dark earth, now leaned against the white picket fence for support. Purple phlox started to appear along the sides.

Every day, my sister Esther called from Ireland. Esther and Deirdre were close. On the Monday after Deirdre got home, she talked to Esther for half an hour. It was unusual for Deirdre to divulge her emotions to anyone outside her immediate family, but Esther was anxious about Deirdre and seized the opportunity to question her assiduously. Eventually Deirdre opened up her heart to her. After she put the phone down, Deirdre had a wide grin on her face.

"That Esther has a way of getting things out of you," she laughed. "She asked me, 'How are you now, Deirdre? Do you have much pain? Do you get out much? Tell me now, Deirdre, do you feel a bit down with all that's going on?' But she made me feel good. I can't wait for her to come over." Esther was due to come in nine days, on Sunday, May 18.

———

Deirdre's friends Katie Swift and Sarah Goulding came to visit. Katie studied at the National Theatre School in Montreal, and Sarah studied Homeopathic Medicine in Toronto. All three of them had developed a strong friendship when they'd lived together in residence during their first year at the University of King's College in Halifax. During the subsequent few years they shared various apartments throughout the city and they spent a summer in Yellowknife together. Katie had long dark hair, but when she learned about Deirdre's illness she had it cut short and donated the long strands to the Canadian Cancer Society to help make wigs.

Sarah stayed around Halifax for a week, visiting Deirdre every day and taking her for short drives. On Wednesday afternoon, after Sarah left for a while, Katie and Deirdre watched a movie in the room upstairs.

I noticed Katie ran up and down the stairs as if she were training for a triathlon. She carried food and dirty dishes back and forth to the kitchen. At one point I went into the room just before Katie arrived with a bowl of hot vegetable chili. Deirdre lay across the love seat, her feet propped up on the opposite arm, looking like a queen bee.

"My goodness, Katie," I said as Katie joined us, "Deirdre has you run ragged."

"Oh that's all right," Deirdre quipped, flicking her hand towards Katie. "She *loves* being my servant." Katie's small face lit up with a wide smile that embellished her dimples.

It rained for a few days, making the air cool and damp. The grass and the leaves on the maple trees were a fresh and luscious emerald green from the moistness. Deirdre complained that her head was cold. I found a purple, round knitted hat that I had bought for a dollar a few months back. Deirdre tried it on and wore it most of the time after that.

During the last five days before she returned to hospital, Deirdre thrived on the activity that prevailed around the house. There was a constant flow of visitors, lively conversations, music from the radio and CDs, and an abundance of competitors for her next board game. When asked about her time in hospital, her reply was always, "Oh, I don't remember much. I was too drugged out."

I enjoyed the vitality of the young people. Their company gave me a sense of optimism, enhancing my faith in the future and in Deirdre's eventual recovery.

By now, she had resigned herself to the reality of never returning to Japan. After she'd recovered from the initial jolt when she arrived home from the hospital, her acceptance was augmented by the support of friends and family here.

One day she told me that she was okay with not going back to Japan again. The latest plan was to have Daichi come and live in Canada. I agreed that it was a possibility but advised her to wait until after the transplant before looking into anything. Inside, I told myself to think only about today, and I sent a request to my spirit for guidance.

On one or two occasions, for short moments, worries about the future penetrated my mind. *How would I cope long-term as Deirdre's sole caregiver?* Right now I was prepared to dedicate the rest of my life to her, but would I always be healthy enough to do that? How would Deirdre cope with the long recovery period and possible relapses? How would Daichi cope with the longevity of the illness and the distance? He was, after all, just twenty-five—very young to persevere through this immense challenge. When my mind began to race like this, I stopped and meditated for a few minutes to bring back balance, surrendering to my spirit, letting go of control; this was Deirdre's journey.

Some mornings she sat on the living room couch, pillows propped behind her back. She stretched her legs out and read, wrote notes, or worked on her laptop, while the guttural sound of the gas flame resonated from beneath the fireplace chimney.

She and Daichi liked to write letters to one another. One day, we walked to a card shop on Quinpool Road, a five-minute walk from the house. After much deliberation, Deirdre chose notepaper that had tiny birds decorating the sides of each page. She wrote to Daichi every day until she became too weak.

She began to read Benazir Bhutto's biography. (Benazir Bhutto was the first and only female Prime Minister of Pakistan, and was assassinated in December of 2007.) Deirdre admired Benazir Bhutto and her vast contribution to human rights. Back in hospital, she continued to read the biography.

While Deirdre was home, Aisling did a project on population health as part of her curriculum. The project entailed promoting careers in health professions to Aboriginal youth, and she needed a brochure for it. Deirdre designed and created one on her Mac laptop.

People who came to visit were surprised by how well she appeared. Her eyes were bright. Her face had some pink in it by now. She ate full meals, and one day she walked from one end of Spring Garden Road to the other, a five-minute walk for healthy people.

But sometimes while she sat on the couch, I noticed a subtle grey-looking area across her lower forehead, just above her eyebrows. Each time my eyes rested on it, I would suddenly feel a sense of dread. *What does this mean? Is this real or am I imagining it?*

Was the untreated lymphoblastic leukemia out of control? Was it something to do with that fungal infection? I knew she hated being scrutinized, so I tried to steal glances from the corner of my eye. At one time, sensing the intensity of my gaze, Deirdre looked up at me with an irritated expression on her face.

"Why are staring at me? It scares me when you look at me like that."

"I was just trying to see if your colour was coming back," I said. After that I tried to stifle the compulsion to study her, but I couldn't resist the occasional quick peek that only served to resurrect my dread.

———————

On Thursday we went to a clothing store. Deirdre got a pair of shoes and a blue dress. She persuaded me to buy red flat shoes and a navy and white dress. Although she could only stay for about twenty minutes, I could tell by her enthusiasm that she enjoyed shopping for her own clothes and relished the sense of independence that it gave her.

After she had settled in at home, I began to go about my normal routine. Every day I walked for an hour, and some days met friends for coffee and lunch. On Saturday evening, while Deirdre stayed at Aisling's apartment, I went to an Irish pub, The Old Triangle, with my friends Mollie and Darlene.

A few years earlier, Deirdre, Aisling, and other dancers used to perform there on St. Patrick's Day morning. They would arrive at 6:00 AM and change into their velvet dresses adorned with Celtic designs. The TV crew from

Breakfast Television would arrive and film them as part of their show that morning.

The pub has ten-foot ceilings and the walls are decorated with photos of Irish poets, old musical instruments, colourful posters, and other artifacts. Stained glass windows engraved with designs of characters from Irish mythology run along two walls. The place holds fond memories of Deirdre's dancing days.

Before Deirdre began to travel she and Aisling belonged to an informal dance troupe, the Blackthorn Dancers. Deirdre helped choreograph most of their dances, sometimes blending Irish music with rock. They performed in different concerts with Natalie McMaster, The Nova Scotia Symphony, and with other well-known artists. A few years ago, the TV network Bravo featured Deirdre and two friends in a documentary about Irish dancing in Halifax. Before she went to Japan, Deirdre and three other dancers did a week's tour with the Celtic group The Barra MacNeils.

Tonight I enjoyed listening to the live Celtic music, the hubbub of activity that surrounded it, and the brief time out where my thoughts wandered away from the surrealism of my life.

Sarah, Deirdre, Katie, Tom, out for a car ride—May 2008

Chapter 16
LATEST BIOPSY RESULTS

Before you were conceived I wanted you
Before you were born I loved you
Before you were here an hour I would die for you
This is the miracle of life.
—Maureen Hawkins

On Friday, May 8, we rose early and prepared to go to Deirdre's bone marrow appointment. Conor drove us to the VG Hospital at 9:30, and dropped us outside the back entrance. We took the elevators to the fourth floor. There was a large square desk in front of the elevators where patients registered for their appointments.

Deirdre filled out the required forms, and a pleasant-looking nurse came and introduced herself. She led us down a corridor to the room where the biopsy would be done. There were rooms off the corridor on either side; some were used as offices. On our right was a long room with eight pink armchairs in a row, each occupied by a patient receiving IV chemo.

As we walked by, we heard the lively conversations between nurses and patients. The corridor was busy with people coming and going.

The nurse led us into a small room that had a sink on the left wall and a stretcher and chair on the right. Deirdre took her coat and shoes off and lay on the stretcher. The nurse took her vital signs and drew blood samples from the hickman line while she asked Deirdre questions about her energy level, pain, appetite, and any other concerns.

Fifteen minutes later Nebojsa arrived, greeting Deirdre in his usual animated manner. He put his arm around her shoulder, and asked her how she was since he last saw her.

"I'm doing well," she said, smiling up at him. "It's really good to be home. I walk a lot and go out for drives, and I even went to the beach one day."

They continued to chat for a while. He said that he would do the biopsy in about an hour when the blood results were back. To do the biopsy, the platelets needed to be at a certain level (low platelets increased the risk of bleeding). She would have a lumbar puncture at 1:00 PM and could go home around 4:00 PM.

When he left, Deirdre climbed onto the stretcher and changed into a gown before the nurse renewed the dressing around the entrance site for the hickman line. After that, I sat beside Deirdre and talked while she waited for Nebojsa to return.

The nurse gave us the blood results. The platelets, white cells, and red cells had increased a lot and, although they were still below normal, they were as high as expected. Deirdre's face lit up as she was buoyed by the good news. Things were going the right way—she would see Dr. White the following Monday. He would let her know the results of the bone marrow biopsy.

Over an hour later, a laboratory technician walked in, pushing a metal trolley carrying lab equipment. She was followed by two medical residents and Nebojsa. When they were ready to begin, I sat facing Deirdre while she lay on her side. Her hip bone was now stronger and less pliable, which made it more difficult to penetrate and manoeuvre the needle through. The procedure bothered her a lot. She grimaced a number of times and squeezed my hand, looking like she was trying to overcome the urge to pull her hip away. After the procedure was successfully completed and the bone marrow samples harvested, she lay flat on her back for an hour, putting pressure on the needle entry site to prevent bleeding.

We went to the cafeteria for lunch. It was busy with staff and visitors lining up to order food at the metal counters, while others waited in line at the cash. After we got our lunch we chose a table by the window. Deirdre had a grilled cheese sandwich and I had a club wrap.

When we returned to the room at 1:00 PM, Aisling was waiting by the door. She had a couple of hours to spare between classes. A medical resident came to do the LP. Deirdre sat on the side of the stretcher, leaning her arms and shoulders across a bedside table, her waist bent, while Aisling and I stood facing her. She tolerated the procedure well, and before completion, the resident gave her a dose of methotrexate through the LP needle. She lay flat for a while afterwards. Aisling returned to her classes.

While Deirdre lay on the stretcher, she asked me to leave the door open. There was a constant flow of people passing by the room. The transplant coordinator nurse was walking by, saw Deirdre, and came into the room. After she asked Deirdre about herself, Deirdre wanted to know if there was any news on a donor.

The nurse was not allowed to disclose information. Taciturn, she assured Deirdre that her name was high on the emergency list, and that they were doing their utmost to find a donor. This bit of information, although obscure, was enough to reassure Deirdre.

"That's really good," she said after the nurse left. "It sounds like they'll have one soon."

"Yeah, it seems like it," I said, as a sudden sense of foreboding came over me.

At 4:00 PM, Conor picked us up outside the hospital. I extended the front seat of the car so that Deirdre could lie flat during the drive home—a precaution to prevent her from getting a headache. When we got in the house, she lay on the couch and read. Later, Aisling and her friends came over and watched a movie with her.

On Saturday morning when I woke up, the sun's bright light penetrated through the curtain on my bedroom window. The birds chirped enthusiastically, making different sounds, each one taking its turn to sing a tune. Their music enhanced the pleasure that the radiance of the morning sun instilled in me.

Deirdre and I got up, went downstairs, called Aisling, and arranged to meet her for coffee at Steve O Reno's. After we got there, Deirdre ordered a blueberry muffin. Aisling had an English muffin with egg and cheese, and I had an apricot scone. We sat and ate, washing our food down with coffee.

A few people came over and chatted with us. They said they were surprised by how great Deirdre was doing, and how well she looked, especially when she displayed her bright eyes and radiant smile.

The wooden chairs were hard on her thin, bony back. Twenty minutes later, after she complained about feeling uncomfortable, we left for the waterfront, a three-minute drive away.

We strolled along the boardwalk for fifteen minutes. The water was motionless, like ice, and glistened against the sun's rays. The smell of the salt air forced me to breathe deeply through my nostrils, and I could almost taste the salty moisture.

Deirdre talked a lot. She glanced all around with a look of contentment on her face. She spoke about the summer when she and her friends had buskered along here. The tall ships were in the harbour then and sometimes the crew from some of the ships invited Deirdre and her friends on board for lunch. The girls had danced to the accompaniment of fiddle tunes played by another friend.

After we left the boardwalk we drove to Aisling's apartment, just off

Spring Garden Road. The city had that air of *joie de vivre*. The sun brightened up the streets, making everything lighter and creating a sense that summer was just ahead. The sidewalks were full of people with happy faces, some dressed in T-shirts and shorts. Girls wore colourful dresses and flip flops. Deirdre wore a beige dress, a cardigan, and a bandana on her head. The baldness at the back of her head was visible under the bandana. When some people noticed, they looked at her thin body and then quickly averted their gaze, unnerved; a reminder of their vulnerability, their mortality.

Every day at 6:00 PM, Deirdre's friends from the community college arrived with supper. They brought homemade pizza, stir fry, salad, haddock, and other dishes. They would stay and chat with Deirdre for a while. Once a week, our friend Fiona dropped off a double-layered, fluffy sponge cake that had strawberries and cream in the middle, and icing sugar on top. Aisling's friend Kate brought us homemade soup on a regular basis.

On Mother's Day, Sunday, May 11, the rain fell incessantly and made for a damp, cool day. Deirdre wore her heavy green coat and purple hat when she, Aisling, Conor, and I went to the Argyle for lunch. As soon as Aisling stopped the car outside the building, I jumped out, opened an umbrella, and held it over Deirdre as she stepped from the car onto the sidewalk and into the restaurant.

We sat in a booth at the back of the restaurant. Deirdre and I had goat cheese pizza—Deirdre had introduced me to this a few years earlier. Conor had Alfredo chicken pasta with bow tie noodles in a cream sauce, and Aisling had a vegetable wrap. For dessert, we shared two slices of chocolate cheesecake.

After we finished eating, Aisling pulled a bag from under the table and handed me a gift-wrapped box. It contained a set of pale green dishes: four mugs, soup bowls, large plates; and a Mother's Day card. Conor said he picked out the card. Aisling and Deirdre had selected the dishes the evening before. I felt warm inside, happy that Deirdre was out of hospital and that we could be together today; a Mother's Day that will always remain etched in my mind.

On Monday, Deirdre and I went to the eighth floor of the VG to meet with Dr. White. As we drove there, Deirdre was full of optimism; the blood results on Friday had been good. She was hopeful the biopsy report would be as positive.

"I hope the news will be good," she said. "Maybe the other kind of leukemia is in remission as well?"

"We'll soon know," I said.

When we got to the office, a nurse dressed in ordinary street clothes greeted us. She took Deirdre's vital signs and enquired about her health. Ten minutes later, Dr. White walked in. With a warm smile on his face, he shook our hands and asked Deirdre how she was. He sat on a chair opposite us.

"Have you enjoyed your time at home?" he asked Deirdre by way of preamble.

Deirdre smiled, looked straight at him and told him how nice it was to be home, "almost back to normal."

After a little while, he spoke frankly as he gave us the biopsy results.

The lymphoblastic leukemia was spreading rapidly.

Deirdre needed chemo treatment immediately. Her blood counts were now high enough, and her organs healthy enough, to withstand the next round of the potent chemo drugs. He would try to get her a bed for the following morning on 8A, the hematology ward directly down the corridor from 8B. Beds were very scarce. If none were available the following morning, they would have one by Wednesday.

"We need to start treatment sooner rather than later," he said, his tone ominous.

He said he would be away for the next month and another hematologist would be taking over for him. As he walked out the door to look for a bed, he had a look of resolve on his face. The nurse said they would call and let us know when they found one.

I could feel Deirdre's fear and disappointment as she sat silently on the chair next to me. Before we left the office, she forced a smile and nodded as a way of saying good-bye to the nurse.

Deirdre's eyes began to gloss over when we got outside the office. I put my arm around her waist and she asked to go home right away. As we made our way down to the main floor in the crowded elevator, she focused on the floor, kept her hands in her pockets, and remained silent. When we got in the car, tears fell freely down her cheeks.

"I was just getting used to being at home and now I have to go back in there again," she said between sobs.

"I know it's awful, Deirdre," I said, my arm around her shoulder. "I'm disappointed as well, but we knew you'd have to come back again. It's another adjustment and another new treatment, but it won't be as bad as the last time. You're not as sick, and remember it's another step forward to recovery."

"I know what you mean," she said, sniffling and wiping away the tears with a Kleenex. "But I'm still disappointed and scared."

"Things will turn out all right in the end," I said as I gave her shoulder a gentle squeeze. I switched on the car engine and headed for home. Even though I was aware that the lymphoblastic leukemia needed to be treated,

I was saddened that Deirdre had to return to hospital just when she had adjusted to life outside.

As soon as we got home she called Daichi and left him a message. Shortly after that, we got the call; there was a bed for Deirdre and she was told to come in at 10:00 the following morning.

I talked to her some more and encouraged to think about how much closer she was to the recovery stage. When she eventually got her mind around the idea of going back to the hospital, she swallowed her disappointment and began to cheer up. After Daichi called back she seemed much happier.

Aisling came to visit and wanted to know the biopsy results. While Deirdre was talking on the phone, Aisling told me she was worried about Deirdre and how she was going to get through all this. I tried to reassure her and encouraged her to think about today only.

Later, Aisling took Deirdre for a drive to her apartment. Deirdre found more clothes in Aisling's closet. She planned to wear them when she came home from hospital again.

Chapter *17*

BACK IN HOSPITAL

Nothing in life is to be feared. It is only to be understood.
—Marie Curie

On Tuesday, May 13, at 10:00 AM, Aisling and I accompanied Deirdre to the hospital. On the way there, she rambled a lot, as though she was trying to dispel her anxiety.

"I'm so scared," she said. "I wonder what my room will be like this time. I wonder if I'll have my own room. I hope they have the Internet."

We went to admitting on the tenth floor. After waiting a little while, Deirdre's name was called and a clerk led us into an office where Deirdre's admission papers were filled in. Fifteen minutes later a lady escorted us to 8A.

Deirdre's face lit up when she saw the familiar faces of some of the nurses from 8B. They greeted her enthusiastically, enquiring about her time at home and complimenting her on her appearance. One of them led us to Deirdre's new room.

The room was halfway down the ward corridor on the right. Just inside the room to the left was a bathroom with a sink and toilet. The room was furnished with a bed, TV, bedside table, locker, big armchair, a small hospital chair, and a bulletin board that hung on the wall facing the foot of the bed. To the left of the bed there was a large window, which looked onto houses, tree-lined streets, and part of the harbour. Deirdre said she liked the brightness of the room.

She looked around, deciding where she could put her things, as though it was her new apartment. She placed pictures of her and Daichi on the window ledge, put her computer on the bedside table, hung small colourful pictures on the bulletin board, and placed her other belongings in the locker. She put notepaper and pens into in a tiny drawer that pulled out from under the bedside table. She also hid two bags of Starburst red chewy candy in there.

Aisling looked happier and left to attend classes, relieved that Deirdre was more content.

There was a kitchen across the corridor from Deirdre's room. It was equipped with a fridge, microwave, table and chairs, toaster oven, kettle, and tea and coffee. Crates of club soda and bottled water were piled against a wall.

Next to the kitchen was the main desk where patients' charts, hospital computers, etc., were kept. This was also the spot where nursing and medical staff came to write reports, exchange reports, and seek out information in their quest to give the utmost in quality care to their patients—patients who put total trust in them to provide healing and comfort.

After the nurse checked Deirdre over, Nebojsa arrived. He welcomed Deirdre back and gave a brief overview of her treatment and the protocol. She could go home to stay that night and the following night. She would have an LP in the afternoon. She would be given a five-day course of allopurinol pills to prevent kidney damage—a side effect of the chemo drugs.

Over the next twenty-nine days she would need ten LPs, one every two to four days, to check the spinal fluid for leukemic cells and to inject the chemo drugs. Cytarabine would be injected with the first five LPs, and methotrexate with the last five. To further protect her kidneys, she would receive large volumes of IV fluids. Blood samples would be sent at least once a day.

The nurse handed us some literature on the protocol; Deirdre ignored it, I read every line. Each drug had different adverse effects. Most caused nausea, vomiting, and severe headaches, but she would receive medication to relieve these symptoms. Deirdre was determined to recover, whatever the cost. She was unperturbed by this information.

After the nurse took blood samples, I accompanied Deirdre to the third floor for a chest X-ray.

That afternoon, Nebojsa did the LP. We went home two hours later, at 5:00 PM. On the way home, Deirdre seemed much happier.

"I feel better now," she said, taking a deep breath after we got in the car. "I just always get so nervous before new things start and when I don't really know what's happening. But now I do."

That evening, Conor took her to a movie called *Iron Man,* where she indulged in popcorn and candies. When they arrived home Conor teased her about the candies that she ate.

"How many of those chewy candies did you have?" he asked, an affectionate smile on his face.

"But they were *so* good." They laughed together.

The following morning, we went back to 8A. Deirdre was started on a twenty-eight-day course of prednisone, a steroid. After she settled into the bed, she was given IV Zofran (she would receive it every twelve hours for five days) and IV Decadron to prevent nausea and vomiting. Thirty minutes later, she received the chemo drugs, vincristine and doxorubicin, through the hickman line.

Before we left the hospital, we called Aisling and arranged to meet for supper at Rogue's Roost, a restaurant on Spring Garden Road. We sat by a window looking out onto the street. We shared two big platefuls of chicken quesadillas and nachos that were covered with cheese, green and red peppers, and tomatoes, with delicious salsa on the side. We chatted about our everyday lives. As other loud conversations went on around us, Deirdre told us she was very relieved to have the second round of chemo underway. She looked happy.

At 6:00 PM Aisling took Deirdre to a free makeup demonstration, organized by the staff at the Sunshine Room, and funded by a bequest from a woman who had died of breast cancer. When they returned home at 8:00, Deirdre's face looked healthy and rosy. She wore blush on her cheeks, dark makeup on her eyes, and had applied pinkish red lipstick. She wore a gold silk bandana with a lion print, an ecru dress with a silk hemline, a black sweater, and tights. She carried a box filled with an array of makeup products, and after the three of us looked through it, Deirdre put it away in her room, to use when she came home again.

On Thursday, we were back at the hospital at 10:00 AM. Deirdre received another IV dose of doxorubicin and later that day, had an LP. She was allowed out for a few hours in the evening. We picked up sushi from a restaurant named Doraku and then called Conor and went to Aisling's apartment, located next door to the restaurant. We ate together before Deirdre and I drove home.

"I'm going to e-mail Dave in Tokyo," she said on the way. "There's a Web site where you can learn Japanese. I could take an online course." She had tried to learn from books and tapes while at home, but couldn't concentrate. 8A did not have wireless Internet but just outside the main door of 8A she could connect to 8B's Internet.

At 10:00 PM, after Deirdre talked to Daichi on Skype, we returned to her room.

Aisling and I began the overnight vigil again. I would stay on weekdays, Aisling on Friday and Saturday. The nurses gave us a cot. We set it up in the only space left in the room, between the foot of the bed and the wall. To get in and out, we had to crawl to the end, but I was grateful to have it. It enabled us to stay with Deirdre at night.

On Friday the sixteenth, at 4:00 AM, the nurse hung a bag of D5W with sodium bicarbonate on the IV pole, connected it to the IV pump tubing, and pushed some buttons on the pump, setting it to run at 250 cc an hour. A number of hours later, she gave a large dose of IV methotrexate. The next day, the IV fluid rate was lowered to 125 cc an hour, and throughout the next week it was adjusted up and down.

A few times a day, Deirdre walked out past the main door of the ward to use the Internet. She would sit on a chair by the wall, flip open her laptop, talk to Daichi on Skype, and do some e-mailing. The nausea, stomach cramps, vomiting, and headaches were starting again, which made it difficult for her to stay there long.

A friend of Deirdre's, Ben Stone, came to visit on Saturday afternoon. She enjoyed Ben's visits. "I get all the news out of him," she said when he left.

At 9:00 PM she received an IV drug called leucovorin, a form of folic acid. It is known as the "rescue drug" because it protects the lining of healthy cells against the ravages of methotrexate. She had about six doses of leucovorin, one every six hours.

The next day she was given the chemo drug asparaginase, which the nurse injected into her hip muscle. That afternoon, even though it was his day off and a long weekend, Nebojsa came to do the LP. He was very concerned about Deirdre.

By now Deirdre understood Nebojsa's accent. They shared jokes and bantered back and forth a lot. One morning the following week, Deirdre leaned forward on the bed, looked out the room door and said, "I wonder why Nebojsa hasn't been in yet today?" A little later, when I saw him going by the room, I shouted to him.

"Hey Nebojsa, you haven't told Deirdre your morning joke." He walked into the room wearing a white lab coat, his face lighting up with laughter. He leaned his hands on the rail at the foot of Deirdre's bed and told her some joke that made her laugh uproariously. I never understood it, despite Deirdre's explanation.

Esther was to arrive that afternoon. Early that morning, I went home and cooked a chicken and broccoli casserole, made a salad, and brought them to the fridge in the ward kitchen to have for supper. Deirdre was excited about Esther's arrival.

It had been three years since they had seen one another. As a child, Deirdre had spent summers in Ireland. Three years ago she had worked in Dublin, not far from the town where Esther lived.

At 4:00 PM Aisling came to stay with Deirdre, and I went to the airport to meet Esther. She walked quickly through security pushing a trolley and dressed in a dark silk skirt, white silk blouse, and a cardigan. Her dark brown hair was shoulder length. She seemed delighted to be here. After a long embrace, she asked about Deirdre and said she couldn't wait to see her. We drove directly to the hospital.

When we got to the room, Deirdre was sitting on a chair, wearing a dress, a cardigan, tights, and her gold bandana. She had applied a little blush on her cheeks. Aisling had helped her get ready.

When Esther saw Deirdre she ran towards her. She hugged her warmly and told her how well she looked.

"Oh my goodness, Deirdre," she said, "I can't get over how great you look. How are you feeling anyway?"

"Not too bad," Deirdre answered, her face beaming. "Thanks for coming to see me. I'm really happy that you came."

After we chatted a while, Esther took some clothes from a bag and handed them to Deirdre and Aisling. They held them out, looked at them, and thanked Esther profusely. Deirdre put hers in the locker, saying she would look at them more later on.

For supper, I put the chicken casserole on plates and heated them in the microwave in the kitchen. We ate together in Deirdre's room, while outside the window the last of the day's sun was settling in below the horizon.

Aisling stayed with Deirdre that night and I drove home with Esther. After she unpacked and settled in, we each had one drink of vodka with 7UP and lemon. It felt cold and fizzy at the back of my throat.

When I called Deirdre at 10:00, they were watching a movie called *Spirited Away* on her laptop. Everything was okay, apart from Deirdre's bouts of nausea and headaches, but she had been medicated for those.

Esther and I chatted until after midnight.

Deirdre after having makeup demonstration—May 2008

Chapter 18
THE BLOOD PATCH

Deep unspeakable suffering may well be called a baptism, a
regeneration, the initiation into a new state. —George Eliot

The following morning, as Esther and I walked to the hospital, the air was
refreshing and moist from the fog. When we got to Deirdre's room, she was
sitting on the side of the bed, eating a bowl of All-Bran with blueberries and
milk. Aisling had prepared her breakfast before leaving for class ten minutes
before. Deirdre smiled when she saw us, asked if we'd slept well, and if we'd
had a little drink before we went to bed. I went and got tea for us all at the
cafeteria. Then Esther and I settled into chairs and chatted for a little while.

A short time later, the doctors came in on rounds and gave a general
update on Deirdre's progress. A chest X-ray done on Friday showed a fungal
infection, *Aspergillus*, in her lung. It could spread throughout the blood and
organs. They prescribed a strong antifungal pill called voriconazole, which
she would have to take for many months. A bronchoscopy was booked for the
following day to glean more information on the infection. For this procedure,
she would be sedated and a tube would be passed down her throat and into
her lungs to obtain specimens for testing.

One day that week while Aisling visited, I went out for coffee with my
friend Carolyn. When I returned, Deirdre was sitting on the side of the bed,
leaning on the bedside table, her face in her hands. Her shoulders shook as
she sobbed quietly. Aisling had her arm around Deirdre's shoulder.

When I asked what was wrong, Deirdre said that an unfamiliar doctor
had explained the possible consequences of the fungal infection.

"I have an infection in my lung and I could end up on a ventilator if I
got a bad flu," she cried.

"Don't let this upset you, Deirdre," I said. "I could be run over by a car when I cross the street tomorrow morning and end up on a ventilator. Who knows what will happen tomorrow?"

She didn't want to hear frank disclosure of frightening possibilities; an explanation of treatment was enough.

"I'm more afraid of the fear itself than when something happens," she said. "I don't want to know about all the bad stuff that might happen."

I spoke to the staff and told them about Deirdre's fear. Always mindful and concerned about her mental as well as physical concerns, they passed the message along to new staff members, who were very respectful of her wishes.

On Tuesday, the nausea and headaches continued. Her neck and back ached. Esther or I would sit on a stool by the side of her bed and rub her neck, back, and stomach, or massage her feet. She was developing the moon-shaped face typical of steroid use.

At 4:00 PM she was taken by stretcher to the X-ray department for the bronchoscopy. I walked alongside. She'd had an Ativan for relaxation before she left. We spent fifteen minutes in the waiting area before the procedure room was ready. The area had a large number of patients on stretchers.

While we waited, I talked to Deirdre about an experience I had when I was twenty-four years old. To renew my Canadian visa, I had a chest X-ray, which revealed a spot in my lung. After numerous tests were negative for TB—including a bronchoscopy—the doctors thought the spot might be cancerous. I had surgery for a lung biopsy and was on a ventilator for a few hours after. I still remember, with perfect clarity, coughing and gagging around that tube. The spot turned out to be a nonreactive TB lesion.

"Here I am, still around after all those years," I said, hoping to reassure her about the future. "I hope these scares don't become a traditional family thing, handed down from mother to daughter. And I didn't get that pleasant sedation before I had the bronchoscopy."

Deirdre smiled, absently rolling Daichi's black cord necklace around her fingers.

The bronchoscopy took about thirty minutes. As she was wheeled from the procedure room, Deirdre was groggy, her eyes half-closed. When she woke up in her room, she said she had no recollection of the bronchoscopy procedure.

Every day, after the sun had burned through the morning fog, it sat majestically in the sky, beaming down its rays, uplifting everything below it. On some of those days, I met friends for coffee or lunch while Esther stayed with Deirdre. It was an opportunity for Esther to lend a hand and spend time alone with her.

Later Deirdre told me that every time she moved, Esther would jump up, determined to provide exactly what Deirdre wanted. Esther felt helpless that she couldn't stay overnight to relieve me, but Deirdre—in almost constant misery—only wanted Aisling or me.

Esther had brought me a book by Marian Keyes, *This Charming Man*, a light read, funny and full of dry wit. Sometimes I would sit on the big armchair by the window, savouring the sun's warmth radiating through the window, and read while Deirdre dozed or read. There was a sleepy quiet in the room. Sometimes I read passages out loud to Deirdre and she would laugh at the familiar Irish humour. I was content with where I was in those moments.

Most mornings, I awoke at 6:00 and enjoyed the silence of the early dawn. I meditated for a little while, asking my spirit and spirit guides to help us through the next few months. Then I tried to leave the future in their hands. I would walk to the bathroom by the elevators. As I walked by, the nurses were always busy, checking vital signs, taking blood samples, giving patient care, and updating patients' charts before the day staff arrived. I would make tea in the kitchen and take it back to the room, and drink it as I read and Deirdre slept.

This was usually when she slept most.

Her appetite was down again but her irresistible penchant for chewy candy, Dairy Queen sundaes, and chocolate remained intact. Though these things aggravated the vomiting, my efforts to persuade her to avoid them were futile. Sometimes while she vomited, her face hanging over the emesis basin, she would look up at me between retching bouts and say, "Ooh, I should have listened to you." Still, all was forgotten at the sight of the next treat.

On Wednesday, she had another LP. The LPs were becoming more uncomfortable for her because of her debilitated state, dehydration, and the side effects of the drugs. Despite maximum anti-pain and anti-nausea medication, sitting upright for the length of time required for the procedure was agonizing for her. This time her face was contorted in pain and discomfort.

By Thursday, the headache was relentless and she was started on a morphine drip. She lay flat most of the time because sitting made the pain and nausea worse. She could not raise her head for more than two or three minutes at a time.

The blood cell counts were falling, as expected. She received platelet and blood transfusions every few days; her organs remained healthy.

I was getting increasingly anxious about the severity and duration of the headaches and felt she had reached the limit of her endurance. A CAT scan, done on Saturday evening, showed no abnormalities. It was decided she must have a cerebral spinal fluid leak (CSF leak). A CSF leak is an escape of fluid that surrounds the spinal cord and brain—an almost unavoidable consequence of numerous LP procedures.

A "blood patch" procedure would be done the next day. Twenty cc of her own blood would be drawn from the hickman line and injected into the same area as the LP injection site—where, it was assumed, the tiny hole lay. After the blood was injected it would form a clot that would seal the hole.

On Sunday morning two nurses, Ann and Jim, came to Deirdre's room and took her by stretcher to the recovery room on the eleventh floor, where the procedure was done. I went with them. Ann and I talked with Deirdre until the doctor arrived fifteen minutes later. I left for an hour and when I returned, Deirdre, lying on her back with the head of the stretcher raised a little, had a radiant smile on her face.

"I wanted to hug that doctor," she said. "When he did that injection, all of a sudden the headache went away. I feel so good now."

A couple of hours later, after we got back to her room, she sat upright and ate a slice of pizza covered with cheese, salami, and mushrooms; she looked like she'd never tasted anything so delicious. Because Esther was leaving that night, Conor and Aisling came to visit and we all had supper in the room.

Tears rolled down Esther's face as she hugged Deirdre good-bye. She planned to return in September when Deirdre would be home. After I dropped her off at the airport I went back to stay with Deirdre for the night.

"I wish I hadn't been so sick when Esther was here," she said sadly.

"You'll see her again in a few months, Deirdre," I said. "The time will go by fast."

Cards and religious icons continued to arrive from friends and relatives; all were praying and trying to help in the way they knew best, with sacred intentions. Deirdre commented on how kind everybody was to her.

On Monday, Ben came to visit again. Ben teaches acting classes, but also works as an actor and runs a theatre company called Zuppa Theatre Company. I stayed in the room while he sat on a chair opposite Deirdre's bed, relating anecdotes about a current play that he was doing and sharing other bits of gossip. Deirdre lay on top of the bed, fully dressed, flinging her head back now and then as she laughed uproariously at Ben's stories.

Despite her suffering, she never lost interest in fashion. When our friend Floria dropped in, Deirdre would crane her neck over the side of the bed, checking out Floria's latest footwear. Floria wore colourful shoes, with three-inch-high, spiky heels, and pointed toes that intrigued Deirdre.

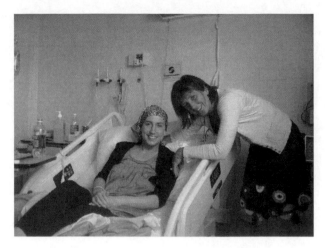

Deirdre and Esther—May 2008

Chapter 19
A New Side Effect

The mind can assert anything and pretend it has proved it. My belief I test on my body, on my intuitional consciousness, and when I get a response there, then I accept. —D.H. Lawrence

On Tuesday, to minimize Deirdre's discomfort, the doctors decided to do the LPs under fluoroscopy—a type of X-ray—from that point on. She was taken to the radiology department, where the procedure would take place. While she lay on her stomach, the fluoroscopy machine took continuous images of her spine that were displayed on a screen. This allowed Nebojsa to view the needle as he inserted it into the correct space. Everything went smoothly.

That afternoon, Deirdre was expecting Ben to visit around 3:00 and I planned to go home for a couple of hours. Just before he arrived she complained of feeling "a bit weird," but she still wanted him to visit. After she encouraged me to go and get some air, I pushed back a feeling that something unusual was happening. I walked home and ten minutes after I got there, rushed back, filled with a sense of urgency I couldn't shake. When I got to the room, Deirdre was sitting on the side of the bed alone, crying and very upset.

"What's wrong, Deirdre?" I asked. "And what happened to Ben?"

"I asked him to leave a little while ago," she said, her voice quivering. "I'm having a stroke. My fingers feel numb and tingly and I can't move them right." She kept exercising the fingers of her left hand—her dominant one. When she squeezed my fingers, both her hands' grips had equal strength and the skin colour was normal, indicating adequate blood supply.

"I think you're just imagining the stroke, Deirdre," I said. "You don't have any weakness in that hand. Maybe you've been confined in the one room for too long. Let's go out in the corridor for a walk. It will clear your mind."

Reluctantly, she agreed. Wanting to see how well she'd grip the IV pole, I encouraged her to push it herself. We walked as far as the main door. Deirdre, her hip bones protruding, moved faster than usual to get it over with. She gripped the IV pole with both her hands and I didn't see any signs of weakness in the left one.

"You held onto the IV pole like you normally would," I said after we got back. "If your left hand were affected by a stroke you would have had difficulty gripping the pole."

"I guess so," she said, looking reassured.

I asked her why she thought she was having a stroke.

"I saw a program on TV about strokes one time," she said. "Tingling and numbness in your fingers is one of the signs."

Half an hour later she was eating an ice cream sundae, using a long-handled, plastic spoon. As she scooped the ice cream up with the spoon, I began to notice she *was* having difficulty grasping the handle. Her long fingers, normally quick and nimble, now moved slowly and awkwardly as she tried to clutch the handle before digging into the creamy mixture. Absorbed in the pleasures of the sundae, she seemed to have forgotten about her fear of a stroke.

My heartbeat picked up speed, bounding against my chest as I continued to study her fingers.

"Maybe we should tell Juliana [the nurse] about that numbness," I said, in an exaggerated matter-of-fact voice. "I'm sure it isn't anything much, probably just a side effect of the drugs, but we'd better let her know anyway." Then, trying to shift my mind away from her fingers, I advised against eating the entire sundae. But it tasted too good; an hour later it landed in the emesis basin.

After I let Juliana know my concern she called the medical resident, who came and examined Deirdre. He couldn't find any problem and attributed the numbness to a side effect of one of the drugs. It would probably pass. Deirdre was happy that she wasn't having a stroke.

I was still worried, thinking about the poor coordination I'd observed in her fingers. It could be a clot or some blockage that came and went, and could eventually lodge in a blood vessel and cause a stroke. During the evening, she complained of numbness a couple of times, and when I checked her finger and hand movements they were normal. She settled and went to sleep around 10:00. I lay awake on the cot, trying to avoid the temptation to check her hand movement.

At 2:00 AM, she woke up and needed to use the washroom. Before I helped her up I checked her hand. When I took it in my hand it was lifeless, with no muscle tone. I lifted her arm up and it fell back on the bed like the arm of a rag doll. Standing beside the bed, I felt the ground tilting beneath me as my legs began to buckle and shake.

I sat on the bed and tried to regain some composure so I could formulate words of comfort. Deirdre looked at me in the semi-darkness and did not say a word. She had a look of painful resignation on her face, as though she had expected this.

"I'm sure the movement will come back again when the effects of the drugs wear off," I said, in a desperate effort to throw her a lifeline of hope and sustain her optimism.

"I knew I was having a stroke," she said in a barely audible whisper, shaking her head. There was no sign of tears.

I pressed the call bell and continued to reassure her, talking nonstop in my husky voice. Juliana came, took Deirdre's vital and neurological signs, and left to call the doctor. She came back wheeling a commode in front of her, and put it by the bed. Deirdre didn't say anything as we helped her up to the commode, carefully supporting her flaccid left arm. When she got back to bed she asked for pain medication, saying her head was pounding. I lifted her arm again, hoping to feel some life in it. There wasn't any.

The resident came, checked her over, and told her she needed a CAT scan right away. She would be taken by ambulance to the Halifax Infirmary Hospital because the VG didn't have technicians on duty at night. It was 2:00 AM and I worried that the ambulance drive would aggravate her litany of discomforts. Deirdre just nodded her head at the resident, too taken up with the headache to care where she went.

I helped her put on tights, socks, and a hospital gown. Half an hour later, Juliana disconnected the IVs from the hickman line and the ambulance attendants arrived. Deirdre sat on the side of the bed, and after I put her limp arm into the sleeve of her coat, she finished putting it on, and lay down on the ambulance stretcher beside the bed. The attendants covered her with blankets and buckled her onto the stretcher. I put her hat on, and Juliana and I walked beside the stretcher to the ambulance waiting outside the main entrance.

Beyond the main door, a light rain was falling. The attendants lifted Deirdre's stretcher into the back of the ambulance. Juliana and I climbed in and sat on a seat beside her. As she lay there on the stretcher, weighing about ninety pounds, she looked fragile and delicate with the hat covering her little head, her tiny face sticking out above the blankets, eyes wide open, and her face draped in acceptance. I wanted to take her in my arms, hold onto her, and protect her forever.

When we got to the Infirmary Hospital, Deirdre said the headache had gone. As she was taken into the CAT scan room, she looked strangely calm. I paced in the waiting room, praying that her arm movement would come back. I pushed the tears back, trying to remain calm and to surrender to my spirit. Thirty minutes later, the door to the X-ray room opened and Deirdre was transferred to the ambulance stretcher. She slept for most of the journey back to her room.

After she was settled back in her bed, she looked pale and exhausted. She said very little before she closed her eyes and slept for a few hours.

I lay awake, drinking cups of weak tea, watching the light of the early dawn come through the window. The rest of the morning went by with excruciating slowness.

When the doctors arrived on rounds, Deirdre sat up in bed facing them, an anxious look on her face. The hematologist said the stroke was most likely a side effect of one the chemo drugs. The blood cell counts were at the bottom and should start to rise within the next couple of days. He booked her for an MRI within the next couple of hours. She was started on an anticoagulant medication, heparin, to prevent blood clots from forming, and Decadron to temporarily decrease brain swelling.

After they left the room, Deirdre called Daichi and told him about the stroke—she could no longer go down the corridor to e-mail or go on Skype. After she put the phone down, she said that Daichi was coming to visit in July. He would be here for her birthday.

"That lifted my spirits," she said, a wide smile on her face.

A short time later we went to the radiology department for the MRI. While we waited outside she talked about her hope that the movement in her arm would come back.

"Maybe they'll find something in the MRI that they can treat," she said.

"At least your left leg wasn't affected," I said. "It wasn't a big stroke."

I waited outside the X-ray room while the MRI was done. John Heelan, a radiologist from Ireland, came and sat with me for a while. Deirdre had taught his daughter Irish dancing a number of years before. He gave me some words of comfort before he was called away to do his next procedure.

An hour later Deirdre emerged from the MRI room, looking agitated and uncomfortable. She said her head ached and she felt nauseated. When she got back to her room, the nurses quickly connected the IV tubing to the hickman line and injected pain and anti-nausea medication into the IV port. Deirdre drifted off to sleep.

Aisling had a class that morning and I hadn't told her about the stroke. I planned to call her after her class was over, but she dropped in unexpectedly on her way home. By that time, Deirdre had woken up and was sitting up in the bed.

"Guess what, Aisling?" Deirdre said, lifting her limp arm and putting it on display. "I had a stroke last night and I can't move my arm. But they think it's from the drugs and I'll get the movement back when they wear off."

Aisling stood motionless; her face looked frozen. She quickly recovered her self-control and walked to the bedside to look at Deirdre's arm.

"What time did that happen?" she asked, her raspy voice revealing her anxiety.

"In the middle of the night," Deirdre said. She continued to recount the events of the night and tried to reassure Aisling that the movement would come back when the effects of the drugs wore off. I reinforced Deirdre's assurances by agreeing with her.

Aisling eventually looked more relaxed.

Later in the afternoon, while walking back from the bathroom, Deirdre stopped, leaned towards her left side and let her shoulder relax so that her limp arm dangled in midair.

"Look at it," she said matter-of-factly as she dangled it like it was some new toy to play with. "It's just like a noodle." Then, with her right hand, she opened the drawer under the bedside table, put a chewy candy in her mouth, picked up her book, and settled back against the pillows to read.

On Thursday morning around 3:00, I helped Deirdre up to the commode. When she went to stand up to go back to bed, her left leg collapsed beneath her. She cried out, terrified, frustrated, and angry as she tried unsuccessfully to put weight on it. Her leg hung from her hip, just like her arm—totally limp.

A cold and naked fear gnawed at my heartstrings. My throat felt like it was closing in as Deirdre lay her head on my shoulder and began to sob unrestrainedly. I dropped all pretense of optimism, no longer able to hold back the flood of tears as I pressed the nurses' call bell.

Chapter 20
A Question of Life Support

My candle burns at both ends;
It will not last the night;
But ah, my foes, and oh, my friends—
It gives a lovely light.
—Edna St. Vincent Millay

In a quivering voice, I told Juliana what had happened while we worked together to get Deirdre back in bed. When Juliana left to call the doctor, I sat on the bed and put my arms around Deirdre. I found some words of encouragement again.

"Don't give up, love," I said. "They'll have the MRI results today and I'm sure there will be some medication to treat whatever is causing these strokes."

"My head is aching," she said, putting her hand over her forehead, and rubbing the tears from her cheeks. Juliana gave her a Dilaudid pill for pain and Zofran for the nausea.

The doctor examined her; there wasn't anything more that could be done until morning. They would decide on the next plan during doctors' rounds. Juliana injected a dose of IV Decadron to decrease the swelling in the brain. A few minutes later I became excited when Deirdre, using her affected left hand, squeezed my hand a couple of times; a ray of hope.

The Dilaudid, a heavy narcotic, helped her sleep for a few hours. I lay on the cot motionless, close to psychotic paralysis.

At 8:00 AM, Aisling arrived on her way to class. She stayed for the rest of the day. I tried to soften the latest news about Deirdre and assured her the paralysis was probably temporary. She sat on Deirdre's bed, joking with her. Occasionally her eyes betrayed her emotions with a fleeting terrified look.

The doctors gave us the results of the MRI. They had consulted the neuro-oncology specialists and were waiting to hear from them. There were lesions (damaged areas) in one of the lobes of the brain—the parietal lobe—that might have been caused by a side effect of a drug or from an infiltrate of leukemic cells. The chemo drugs injected into the spinal fluid do not cross the brain barrier, and would not prevent the infiltration of leukemic cells to the brain itself. There was talk of brain radiation, but the depleted blood cell count would add more dangers to the already high risks that came with radiation.

While the doctors spoke, Deirdre sat upright in the bed, eyes bright, her head turned away from them.

"I'm sorry I couldn't look straight at you," she said with a smile as they were leaving. Immediately after they left I stood beside the bed and asked her to look at me; she turned and looked me straight in the eye. I never did find out if she was being mischievous or if her brain was off course.

Half an hour later Deirdre lay on her side, sleeping. Tracey, Deirdre's nurse that day, came and sat beside me. She put her arm around my shoulder while I allowed my tears to fall.

"I wish that I was the one in the bed," I said, looking at Deirdre. Deirdre half-opened her eyes and with a little smile gave me a knowing look.

"But Deirdre knows that," I said.

Aisling encouraged me to go home and get some sleep.

Walking home, the chill of the dawn gave way to the warmth of the sun that was making its way higher in the sky. I prayed, still hopeful, pleading for a miracle. After I got in the door, I called Conor and told him about Deirdre, trying to make the news sound less ominous. He would come to the hospital later.

I sent an e-mail to Esther. An hour later, unable to sleep, I got up and left to go back to the hospital.

About halfway there, I was standing in front of a red traffic light, waiting to cross the road. As I looked ahead, mindlessly, a sudden thought came to me: Deirdre was not going to live and I had to let her go.

The thought no longer terrified me; it was as if suddenly something inside me opened up, allowing me to surrender and accept Deirdre's inevitable passing.

Numbed by the revelation, I prayed that she wouldn't suffer anymore. An immense sadness filled me. Tears fell on my cheeks underneath my dark sunglasses as I continued on my way to the hospital.

At 11:30, when I arrived at the ward, one of the nurses told me that Deirdre was down in the radiology department having an LP. I immediately took the elevator to the department, but when I got there, I was told that she had just been taken back to the ward. When I got to her room, Deirdre lay flat in bed, her eyelids heavy, looking like she was about to sink into a deep sleep.

Later, Aisling told me that while she waited outside the X-ray room for Deirdre, a staff member came and asked her to go inside. When she entered the X-ray room, Deirdre was shaking uncontrollably. Still terrified from the fallout of the stroke, the move from the stretcher to the X-ray table and having to lie on her stomach had stretched her to the limit. She had been given Ativan. Aisling stayed with her for the rest of the procedure.

When Nebojsa finished the procedure, rather than wait for a porter to take Deirdre back to her room, he told Aisling to grab one end of the stretcher and the two of them wheeled her back up right away.

She slept for an hour and when she awoke, she asked for a sausage sandwich from Tim Hortons. While Aisling went to get the sandwich, she called Daichi and told him what had happened. After she put the phone down, her eyes looked bright with delight.

"Daichi is coming to visit and he'll be here on Monday," she said.

Aisling returned with the sandwich—a biscuit with a sausage in between. Deirdre sat upright in the bed, holding the sandwich in her right hand.

"I feel like I'm in an opium den," she said, eyes wide and smiling—she had been without pain medication for a few hours.

"How do you know what it feels like to be in an opium den?" I asked jokingly.

"I saw a program about it on TV," she answered. "That sandwich was so good." Holding onto the sandwich between the fingers and thumb of her right hand, she held it aloft, above her forehead.

"You still have some, Deirdre," Aisling said.

"Oh yeah, I forgot," she said, bringing her hand down to eye level. She looked at the remainder of the sandwich before she took another bite. She repeated the same scenario four more times and each time Aisling reminded her that she still had some. She continued to entertain us with her witty remarks, making us laugh so hard that we forgot about the nightmare that was happening.

A little while later, the phone on the bedside table rang and Aisling answered. When she said "Hi, Ben," Deirdre turned her head toward the phone.

"Tell him he stroked me out the other day," she shouted, laughing loudly while Aisling handed her the receiver.

Before she put the receiver back down, she said "Bye, Strokey," in a soft, playful tone.

Her speech was as articulate as ever. After she talked to Ben she said, "I'll write to him. No, I mean e-mail him." She shook her head, a momentary worried look on her face, as if she were surprised by this tiny slip in her words.

Later, Margie Whitehouse, one of the nurses, told me that Deirdre had said she would challenge the nurses to a wheelchair race up and down the corridor. As she continued to joke with Margie, she said that she would have to live in a country where they didn't use eating utensils, now that she could only use one hand.

Around 3:00 PM, my friend Anastazia came with a large colourful artificial lily, Belgian chocolates, and a pink bracelet with tiny beads. The bracelet had a medal that hung on the end. Deirdre normally didn't wear religious icons, but she put the bracelet around her wrist, and gave it an admiring look after she thanked Anastazia.

Just after Anastazia left, two young physiotherapists came and helped Deirdre sit on the side of the bed. They showed her some exercises and Deirdre politely followed their instructions. After they left she said she hoped she wouldn't have to do that every day.

I went to the cafeteria and got a coffee. Later Aisling told me that Deirdre ate a few Belgian chocolates and Reese's Pieces while I was away.

She never did get the dreaded mouth sores, despite the amount of junk food that she ate

At 4:00 PM, the radiation oncologist came to see Deirdre. A small man with a pleasant smile, he introduced himself, sat on the bed facing Deirdre, and looked at her from behind his gold-rimmed glasses.

Deirdre sat upright, looked straight at him, and flashed her smile. Her eyes were bright under her long eyelashes. Aisling and I stood on either side of the bed.

In a soft, steady voice he began to explain the next treatment.

The leukemic cells had infiltrated the parietal lobe of her brain and the swelling was significant. The hematology staff, neuro-oncologists, radiation oncologists, and medical staff in a Boston hospital had collaborated and decided that, despite the low blood counts, brain radiation treatment was crucial and needed to be done immediately to decrease the swelling. The risks of radiation were extremely dangerous. He listed some of them. One was mental slowdown.

"That would be temporary?" I asked.

"No. Permanent," he answered.

Deirdre was booked for 9:00 the following morning, to be fitted for a special mask that would be moulded to suit her head and face. The mask would allow precision in treating only the affected areas of her brain.

"The radiation will take the swelling down," Deirdre said, smiling at him. "That will be good because then I'll be able to use my arm and leg again."

He nodded in agreement.

Mercifully, there was little time to contemplate the immensity of the information we'd just been given. Our sense of reality and rationality had left us.

Since I'd arrived back in the hospital, I hadn't thought about my revelation earlier in the day. Right after the oncologist left, Deirdre complained of a severe headache.

"I feel like there's a knife going through my head," she said, pointing to her forehead. Tracey gave her a Dilaudid pill. Before it had time to take effect, Deirdre was slurring her words as she lay back against the pillow and went into a deep sleep.

The afternoon that my mother passed on, I was also sitting beside her bed. She had pointed to her chest and said, "I feel like there's a knife going through my chest." She was experiencing chest pain from a heart attack. Today, when Deirdre said these almost identical words, I immediately sensed that she was going to pass on that night.

A little while later, I noticed her bladder was swollen. She was no longer capable of using a bedpan and Tracey inserted a urine catheter.

At 5:45 PM, Deirdre was sleeping and Aisling had gone out for a while. I slipped into the kitchen to make a cup of tea. Five minutes later, when I was about to return to the room, the hematologist who was on that day walked past the kitchen on his way home. He stopped to talk to me.

"There's only a very slim chance that she'll make it through this," he said. "Her brain could cone with all that swelling."

"If that happens, I'd rather you didn't intubate her," I said.

He said that they would probably have to intubate and take her to the ICU. A decision would be made there on the next course of treatment. Brain coning (herniation) is the deadly result of excessive brain swelling. The brain structures shift within the skull, causing downward pressure. Blood and oxygen supplies diminish; finally cell death occurs. In Deirdre's case, if that happened, nothing more could be done for her.

Intubation would involve passing a tube down into her lungs that would be connected to a ventilator—a life support that would not extend Deirdre's life; it would only extend the length of her passing.

Concerned about Deirdre being alone, and without asking any more questions, I went back to her room. She was sitting upright in the bed, leaning forward and vomiting everything she'd eaten that day across the sheets. Her eyes were mostly closed and she nearly toppled to her left side. I ran to her and held her upright. Just then, Aisling arrived in the room.

I pressed the call bell. We held onto Deirdre from either side, our arms around her shoulders. We reassured her and told her how much we loved her, as her head tilted forward toward her chest.

Tracey and another nurse came and cleaned her up. While they were washing her, she lifted her head for a few seconds and looked at them with heavy eyes, a shy half-grin on her face.

"Sorry. Big barf," she said.

After the nurses finished cleaning her, Deirdre lay on her side and continued to sleep. Because I sat close to Deirdre, I didn't get an opportunity to explain to Aisling what the hematologist had told me. Conor came and we sat and talked softly to one another.

"It's not good," I whispered. They nodded knowingly. Tears began to drip from their eyes.

Around 8:00 PM, Deirdre's breathing shifted to a deeper place and her eyes looked heavier. I parted her eyelids; her pupils were fixed and dilated, a major sign of brain injury—possibly coning. When I shook her gently and called her name, she didn't respond.

I quickly explained to Aisling and Conor what the hematologist had said in the kitchen. Aisling went to get Juliana.

I had been prepared for this. Protecting the dignity of Deirdre's passing was now foremost on my mind.

Juliana called the resident, who came and examined Deirdre. The resident said she was going to call the staff doctor on call. Aisling and I followed her to the door and I asked if I could speak to her. I let her know what the hematologist told me.

"I know what brain coning involves," I said. "In Deirdre's case it's irreversible. I've worked in ICUs for twenty-five years and I have a good idea when intubation is worthwhile, when there's a chance of survival. To intubate Deirdre and put her on life support would be inflicting futile pain and suffering on her and on us. Please let her go with the dignity she deserves."

After I talked to her some more, Aisling and I went back into the room, and the three of us sat by the bed. We held Deirdre's hands and talked to her. Although her breathing was heavy, she looked comfortable, as if she were in a deep sleep.

About ten minutes later, the on-call staff hematologist, Dr. Hasegawa, arrived and looked at Deirdre.

"We will leave her here," she said. "Nothing more will be done."

I felt my mind and body lighten as the heavy burden of responsibility was taken from me. The dignity of Deirdre's passing was secured.

We continued to sit by the bedside while Deirdre breathed peacefully, in a comatose state, medication no longer required. She lay on her side with the head of the bed raised—dressed in a hospital gown, her face peaceful, eyebrows and long eyelashes still there, her head bald and beautiful—still having that full experience.

As the hours went by, friends came and went. Tears fell continuously as we talked and laughed about Deirdre, just as she would have wanted it. Without too much "melodrama," as she would say, her spirit choosing to change form late at night when the world around was quiet, making the transition calm and peaceful. We took turns holding her hands, kissing her soft cheeks, embracing her.

Aisling called Daichi. He would arrive on Sunday.

For the last couple of hours, an air of beautiful serenity—a sacred atmosphere—filled the room, emanating from Deirdre.

It felt as though she had become immersed in some beautiful kind of love. Later I read that sometimes a person's soul will leave the body before they pass over, staying around to help their loved ones.

At 1:25 AM, the pause between her breaths increased. She breathed her last breath at 1:30 AM on Friday, May 30, as she returned gracefully and fluidly to the realm of life that she had come from; in the same style that she entered this life; in the same style that she lived her short life.

At 2:00 AM, we reluctantly said good-bye to Deirdre and walked away quietly, letting our tears fall freely.

Aisling and Conor stayed with me that night. I called Esther before I went to bed. Although she was aware of how sick Deirdre had been the day before, she said she felt numb. She would arrive in Halifax the next day.

Chapter 21

PREPARATIONS FOR THE CELEBRATION

A good heart is better than all the heads in the world. —Edward Bulwer-Lytton

On Friday morning I awoke at 8:00 AM after sleeping for a few hours. I prayed to Deirdre, letting her know that I was aware of her presence, asking her to help us in whatever way she could.

I went down to the kitchen and made tea and toast, and a short while later, Aisling and Conor joined me. We talked for a little while before Conor had to leave. Nebojsa called from the hospital offering his condolences, telling Aisling she had to "live a big life for two people." He said he was happy that Deirdre didn't suffer more; I could tell by his tone that he was very sad.

Aisling and I sat on the back deck until midday. As the sun warmed the air around us, we talked nonstop about Deirdre, recounting anecdotes of her younger years, how much joy she brought to us, and how lucky we were to have had her for twenty-five years. We talked about how funny she had been the day before—her last day in human form. Her humour, even then a gift to us from her spirit, setting us at ease as she still played the role as the comic relief, still not missing the moment, the beauty of "now."

Throughout the rest of the day, friends came and went. They brought food and flowers and offered their help. I talked about Deirdre, told stories about her, and felt her presence.

Aisling stayed that night, Friday.

The next morning, when I awoke after six hours of sleep, I was surprised by how well I'd slept. Aisling said she had slept well.

I couldn't evade funeral arrangements any longer. Thoughts of it frightened me. I had to curb some resentment at having to do this for my daughter. It wasn't supposed to be like this. Things were all askew. She should be making my funeral arrangements.

After I rested and meditated, I realized that I didn't have the right to control Deirdre's life's journey. I had to accept it and support her, as always.

I had very limited knowledge about funerals and had gone to very few. I prayed to Deirdre, asking for direction. Aisling and I agreed on cremation. I spoke to a friend who recommended a cremation service, and after I called and discussed things with them, they agreed to look after it all. I knew that Deirdre would not want to be viewed—if she minded being stared at when she was sick, she certainly wouldn't want to be on display like "an artifact in a museum" now.

Where would we put her ashes?

We didn't have to think long about that. The beach. The beach where the labour pains that signalled her birth had started; the beach where on beautiful summer days she had played as a child; the beach where she had played with friends as an adult. Rainbow Haven.

What would she want for a funeral service?

During her childhood, we went to St. Peter's, a church in Dartmouth. Deirdre had been an altar girl there for a few years. Although she was no longer a practising Catholic, the church had been part of her formative years. I called the parish priest and we arranged to meet about readings and songs for the service.

We were having difficulty deciding on an obituary photograph. On Sunday morning, I looked at a picture that Daichi had taken the night before she left Japan. In it, she was standing in front of a fridge, drinking from a large juice container. I thought of how much this photo depicted her personality—funny, mischievous, daring—but perhaps not suitable for the obituary. An hour later, Aisling woke and came downstairs.

She stood and looked at the picture.

"I think this might be a good obituary picture," she said without prompting.

"That's it," I said. "Deirdre has told us. This is what we'll put in."

As the sun shone through the patio doors, I sat in front of the dining table and started to write her obituary note. After I settled with pen and paper and focused my mind on Deirdre, my fingers and pen moved across and down the page, not stopping until I had written down my loving thoughts and memories of her.

Aisling added some of her thoughts before we submitted it for publication.

Esther and my brother Jimmy arrived on Saturday afternoon. Esther said she was still finding it hard to comprehend. She remembered Deirdre savouring a slice of pizza less than a week ago, and now—

Esther worried about us, especially about me, but I assured her that Deirdre was helping me. She offered me sleeping pills. I refused; maybe I'd need them later. Despite the sadness, I was surprised by how strong I felt.

My brother Mossie, a priest, arrived from Ireland on Sunday, surprising us with his visit. He hadn't been in Nova Scotia for about twenty-six years. He stayed with friends, Jill and Bob, whom he had known for many years.

Aisling and I met with Deirdre's friend Aisling Chin Yee and Father Richards, the priest at St. Peter's. He gave us readings and prayers from which to choose. We had planned that Aisling Chin Yee and Katie Swift would do a tribute to Deirdre at the service. It was against the rules of the Catholic Church to do a tribute during the Mass, so Father Richards kindly let them do a five-minute talk before the Mass began.

Knowing how important Deirdre's friends were to her, I had asked them to do the church service arrangements. They conferred with me about the readings and songs.

On Monday afternoon hymn books, papers, flowers, and pictures of Deirdre covered my dining table and whatever other horizontal spaces were available nearby. Ben, Graeme, Peter Smith, Susan, Aisling Chin Yee, Katie, Alex, and Aisling sat around the table and spent a couple of hours planning the songs and prayers. They also decided on the pictures and flowers for Deirdre's memorial service.

There was another hubbub of activity outside on the deck, where some of Aisling's friends worked vigorously, making flower arrangements for the church. The flowers were all over the deck, waiting to be put in the twenty vases. People brought lawn chairs and bottles of wine to the house for the reception the next day.

The funeral Mass would be at 10:00 on Tuesday morning. It rained most of Sunday and Monday. I chose to have a reception at my house after the funeral; Deirdre would want it here. I hoped for a sunny day but didn't worry about it. I knew everything would fall into place.

Daichi arrived on Sunday evening, looking emotionally and physically exhausted. We talked and cried for a while. He had a bowl of shrimp casserole and then went to bed. Before he left Japan, he had called and asked me that Deirdre's cremation not take place until he had seen her.

On Monday, Conor, Daichi, Aisling, and I drove to where Deirdre's body was.

When we arrived, a staff person led us into a room where there was a simple wooden coffin. Deirdre lay in there, looking like a porcelain doll, still in the hospital gown, wearing orange lipstick—not her favourite colour. I wondered what witty remark she would have made about the lipstick. The pink beaded bracelet was on her wrist. The four of us stood beside the coffin, tears streaming down our faces.

Daichi took a box from his pocket. He took two silver rings out of it and placed one on Deirdre's ring finger, the other on his. We said good-bye again, and left Daichi alone with her. Fifteen minutes later, when he came out, he had a look of calmness about him.

For most of the journey home, we spoke very little. I asked Daichi if he had heard from Deirdre's friend Dave in Tokyo.

"Oh, yes," he said. "When I talked to her in the room back there, I gave her his messages, and the news about her other friends in Tokyo." He said it as if she were still lying in the hospital bed, eager for all the news from Japan. His innate sense of spirituality was unique. Nothing intellectual, not a concept, but straight from the heart: simple, uncluttered, epitomizing true spirituality.

Chapter 22

THE CELEBRATION

I hope I can love the moment I am in, have a certain excitement and mystery about the future and also appreciate and love my past. —Deirdre's diary, 2002

Our friend Ross Munro drove us to the church on Tuesday. He and his wife Henrietta were Deirdre's godparents. At 9:00 AM, as we drove across the bridge between Halifax and Dartmouth, the sun made its way out between the white clouds that drifted back and forth in the sky above the harbour.

When we arrived at the church, a handful of people had already arrived.

The inside of the church was circular, giving it an expansive feel. Stained glass adorned many of the windows and it had a granite altar in the centre. There were nine sections of pews surrounding it. We sat in one that was close to the altar.

Deirdre's and Aisling's friends had gone to the church the evening before and set up the framed pictures of Deirdre and the vases of flowers. The flowers decorated the steps leading up to the altar. Vases of pink and purple flowers added colour and life to areas surrounding the altar and around the church.

A brown jewellery box containing Deirdre's ashes stood on a stand at the top of the steps. Flowers and pictures of Deirdre surrounded it.

A continuous flow of people entered the church. Hundreds of young people sat in the pews around the church circle. Young ladies wore summer silk dresses with floral designs, and some wore colourful suits. Their feet were decorated with silver- or golden-coloured high-heeled sandals and painted toenails. Young men wore dress pants and suits with colourful shirts and ties. Most were close to Deirdre and, it seemed, they dressed to suit her style.

I envisioned Deirdre in the midst of the circle, waiting for her going-away party to begin, her energetic spirit blending in with the energetic tributes that surrounded her. The vibrant fashions, the flowers, the brilliant colours that the sun created as it beamed through the stained glass windows: all complemented the energetic love of everybody there.

As we waited for the Mass to begin, Susan Le Blanc sang Deirdre's favourite song, "Such Great Heights." She slowed the melody down, making it sound like a beautiful hymn. Deirdre had sent Daichi a CD of this song, her first gift to him.

By 10:00, the church was filled with about five hundred people. A sombre silence prevailed. Nobody coughed. Nobody whispered. Aisling Chin Yee and Katie Swift walked to the podium. Aisling, attractive, oriental-looking, was dressed in a black and white dress. Katie, her eyes bright and sparkling, her small face dotted here and there with freckles, wore a dark rose dress. They were both smiling. They began their rendition and celebration of Deirdre, alternating back and forth, their voices strong and full of enthusiasm.

Aisling: I am so lucky. I am so lucky because I shared the greater part of my life with Deirdre. Which means that I spent most of my life laughing. She made being a friend and good person effortless. She was an honest and genuine person who could make any situation fun, entertaining, and incredibly hilarious.

Katie: I can safely and boldly say that I never met anyone like Deirdre. No one even comes close. She was actually *the* weirdest, most hilarious, and the most interesting person I have ever known. From the moment I met her I never quite understood her, and this intrigued me to try and unravel the mystery of Deirdre.

Whenever I tried to explain what my friend Deirdre was like to someone who had never met her, I always felt like words were not enough. No description could ever really do her justice. "Well, you'll just have to meet her," I would usually end up saying.

Eight years, five apartments together, and countless nights at the Marquee Club later, it is precisely that indescribable quality that made me absolutely adore her.

The first time I met Deirdre was from across the hallway on the second floor of Alex Hall, the all-girls' residence at King's College. She was wearing half a shirt, exposing her belly button ring, and she wore a colourful, silky scarf on her head, no doubt covering up her unkempt, streaky blond hair.

In the beginning, everything was mysterious about Deirdre. There was a constant flow of shady-looking characters coming in and out of her dorm.

There was often eerie mist flowing out of her doorway, and the ever-intriguing smell of grilled cheese sandwiches wafted across the hallway into my room.

The intrigue was too much for me. I had to know the mystery that was Deirdre.

Of course I would come to know those shady-looking characters as *Dartmouthians*—a species of humans I had yet to encounter. The mist would prove to be her trusty humidifier, and the grilled cheese sandwiches were simply Deirdre's dissatisfaction with cafeteria food. She took her meals into her own hands.

Aisling: In different cities during university, Deirdre visited me; in Montreal with her dancers, causing antics on St-Laurent Street.

Travelling together, I could leave all the planning up to Deirdre, which meant that she was the one who pointed blindly at the map, rather than me. An adventurer, she would always want to be on the first bus to the next destination, to keep moving, seeing, experiencing as much as we could and living in the "now." It often meant we didn't really look into our exit route, and got stuck in small Greek villages for days, shocking all the locals with our white midriffs and stereotypical North American penchant for copious amounts of Coca-Cola. But if there was anyone who could make a small village filled with goats and old ladies with gold teeth into a party, it was Deirdre.

And like I said, Deirdre lived everything to its fullest, in the "now," and made us all appreciate what we had, sharing that moment, even if it meant forgetting to set an alarm clock and missing our flight to Ireland. But we would always get to where we needed to be in the end, Deirdre-style.

Katie: Deirdre's practicality always astounded me. More often than not, she was chaotically impulsive, and fun incarnate. But if the situation demanded, she could be the most rational of us all. There was a certain unfortunate event involving a broken bottle on Barrington Street, which led to handcuffs and yours truly in the back of a police car. As I sat sobbing, flabbergasted by what was happening, Deirdre was on that police officer like nobody's business. "Where are you taking her? What time will she be out? Will she be in a cell with women? Can't you give us a receipt for her or something?" Important questions that would not have crossed my mind.

"It's okay," she told me, putting her hand against the car window. "I'll come save you. I promise. Stay strong!" she told me as the car pulled away. Of course, she stayed true to her word. Upon my release the next morning, who was waiting for me outside in the pouring rain? None other but a very groggy and excited Deirdre, armed with our friend Aeneas and a video camera, ready and eager to record my humiliation for all to see.

It was as if her humour was beyond her control. It was effortless, and it never seemed to leave her, even during what proved to be the most trying of times.

When I was visiting her a few weeks ago, she had a newfound obsession: the board game Sorry! Anyone she could rope into playing a round with her was doomed. She had secret Sorry! skills, and would antagonize her opponents with little comments under her breath… "Oh…interesting choice." Or a boisterous, "Sarry!" when she drew the coveted card that allowed her to send an opponent back to the starting block. We laughed so hard playing that stupid board game that we both cried. It was as if nothing had changed.

I can't think of a better way to remember her: cracking jokes, making fun of the way I moved my pawn around the board, making fun of the word "pawn," and bringing absolute joy to everyone who was fortunate enough to be around her.

Aisling: We all spent so much of our life around the sea and on beaches. The water was a place to be shared with loved ones, friends. And what brave soul was the first one in the water? Never me…and often Deirdre. Deirdre, who explored her connection to the ocean in her art, from her infamous fish drawings, to her travels around the world, right down to the salted water she used to make her Kraft Dinner.

And when I think of this, my dear friend, through my salty tears, you still make me smile. When I think of what we shared, and the joy you gave to everyone who you met along your journey through life, I am so grateful for knowing you. You shaped me as a person and I know you will always be there for all of us, throughout the rest of our lives, until we see you again.

Author's explanatory notes: The "Dartmouthians" Katie mentioned were people from Dartmouth; Deirdre was one of them. She travelled to Greece with Aisling and in one village a herd of goats ran after Deirdre, providing entertainment for the locals. On their way to Ireland from London, Deirdre set the alarm clock four hours earlier than what it was supposed to be. They arrived at the airport early. The airline let them travel first class—carrying their backpacks and wearing scummy clothes.

And the jail incident: Deirdre, Aeneas, and Katie were walking along Barrington Street one night. Katie, the sober one, was holding a beer bottle, her first drink of the night. When she saw the police, she panicked and threw the bottle into an alleyway between two buildings. The policeman saw her throw it; hence the handcuffing and overnight jailing.

When the two girls finished, the silence was replaced by the sounds of unrestrained laughter. The priests walked from the sacristy and began the Mass. Mossie did the homily, comparing Deirdre to Saint Theresa. Deirdre didn't quite fit the definition of a saint, but she would have smiled at the comparison. Father Richards said a few words about her. People chuckled when he began by saying that the reason he didn't know her well was because "We didn't travel in the same circles," referring to the incident on Barrington Street.

Ben and Graeme read two readings. One was about there being a time for everything. That concurred with my belief that our moment of birth and our moment of death are planned ahead.

This is perhaps one of the reasons why I am free of the anger I might have felt at Deirdre's passing before my own. "To everything…there is a season… and a time for every purpose under heaven. A time to be born, a time to die…"

The final hymn, "Lord of the Dance," so appropriate for Deirdre, caused a flow of tears from her dancing friends and former students.

When the service ended, people waited for us to leave first. I passed the message along to Conor at the end of the pew and we walked outside together, welcomed by the sun pouring out its brilliant rays. We stopped at the bottom of the four steps outside the church and mingled and talked to as many people as possible. Two former dance students of Deirdre's, now sixteen, had been seven-year-olds when Deirdre taught them. They smiled all the time they talked about her. We stayed for close to an hour and most people were still there chatting and laughing with one another when we left—the way Deirdre would have liked it.

When we got home, Barbara, Mollie, Darlene, and Floria were busy in the kitchen preparing the food, wine, beer, tea, and coffee. There was an abundance of everything; chili, fish casseroles, fruit trays, cheese trays, and homemade breads were among the array of food.

In an hour, the kitchen, dining area, family room, back deck, and backyard were filled with people. Flowers were everywhere. Beautiful arrangements filled vases on windowsills, tables, and around the sides of the old baby grand piano in the family room. The thermometer over the back deck read 30°C as the sun beamed down on it. Rain was forecast for the rest of the week, but not a drop fell that day.

Aisling Chin Yee had created a CD with a slide show of Deirdre, showing pictures from her baby years up to when she was in the hospital. It played to the accompaniment of the song "Such Great Heights." We put the TV on the old oak desk in the family room, and after Aisling Chin Yee popped the CD in the DVD player, it played continuously. Most people came in and out to watch it. Aisling posted it on YouTube, where it can still be viewed by typing "Deirdre Porter" in the search box.

Outside in the backyard, the grass competed for space with a plethora of flowering forget-me-nots. They had cropped up over the past few days. Leah, a friend of Aisling's, picked one and put it into a frame for Aisling.

Groups of people, all dressed up, sat on a second deck by the fence at the back of the yard. The branches of a maple tree, in full leaf with the freshness of spring, sheltered them from the sun's hot rays. They ate platefuls of food, and drank wine and beer as they celebrated Deirdre's past and present life.

By midafternoon the majority of people had gone. Most offered to help in whatever way they could. Barbara and Mollie stayed in the kitchen. They continued to serve food and drinks and clean up until almost everybody had headed home.

About thirty people stayed until later that night. Aisling, Conor, and Daichi were in good spirits, chatting with everybody like it was a regular party. Aisling and Conor went back to their own apartments that night. Esther, Jimmy, Daichi, and I went to bed around 10:00, worn out from the day's events. Mossie left earlier to stay with Jill and Bob. I didn't shed any tears that day. My well had dried up over the previous few days.

The first law of physics:
Energy can neither be created nor
destroyed, it can only change form.
What happens to the massive amount
of energy that makes us who we are,
when our bodies cease to function?
The soul. The essence.

Chapter 23
DEIRDRE'S WAY OF COMMUNICATING

My problems are so insignificant compared to everything else that we can't see out there. We only make up such a small portion. We are like particles that make something else; a whole other matter that we don't even know exists. Maybe I am just a big mass of energy, no one sees or hears, but feels. —Deirdre's diary, 2002

On Wednesday morning, fifteen of us went to Rainbow Haven Beach where we spread Deirdre's ashes. The day was mostly damp and rainy, but when we got to the beach the sun peeked through the clouds. The grey-blue ocean rushed and receded as the seagulls cawed above us.

We walked to the water's edge and each of us took a handful of ashes from the thick plastic bag. We opened our hands, and let the wind blow Deirdre's ashes across the beach and over the water. I prayed to her, letting her know again that I was aware of her essence around us, asking that she be part of this ritual.

The ring that Daichi had placed on Deirdre's finger was among the ashes. He took it in his hands, regarded it pensively for a little while, and then tossed it into the water along with some of Deirdre's ashes.

We stayed silent for a while, watching the waves carry Deirdre's old form out into the ocean, like a uniform that is no longer needed—Deirdre's work here completed. As we walked across the firm, moist sand we stopped frequently to look back at her resting place, agreeing this was a perfect spot for her. Then we continued on to the boardwalk, made our way to our cars, and drove home.

Daichi made us *nabe* for supper. With Conor as his assistant, both of them spent most of the afternoon in the kitchen, slicing oysters, leeks, special mushrooms, sausages, clams, cabbages, and other healthy ingredients to add to the pot on the stove. As we sat around the table, Daichi put the pot of piping hot *nabe* in the middle, and we each scooped a ladle or two into our bowls. It tasted scrumptious. Just as we finished, our friend Steve Penny came through the door, serenading us with the sounds of his banjo tune.

On Thursday evening, Esther and I drove Jimmy to the airport to catch his flight back home to Ireland. Esther stayed for another week and Mossie left the following Sunday.

On Friday night, Aisling and Deirdre's friends organized an Irish wake for Deirdre at the Old Triangle Irish Ale House. They had her obituary photo printed on forty T-shirts, and gave them to people to wear that night—they ran out. Jimmy Sweeny and Kevin Roach, musicians who had provided the musical accompaniment for some of Deirdre's dancing gigs, happened to be the entertainment that night. The two dedicated a number of songs to Deirdre.

Esther and I went for an hour and left at 10:30. Most people stayed until 1:00 AM; Deirdre, I'm sure, was among those.

Daichi left on Saturday. I took him to the airport for his 6:00 AM flight. On the way there we agreed that we should all meet again sometime. He said that he could feel Deirdre around him. He would continue to go forward with his life and ask Deirdre's help along the way.

Aisling had deferred writing one of her exams. It had been scheduled the week that Deirdre passed on. She wrote it three weeks later. Her friends Katie Gardener and Sarah Lea also asked permission to defer theirs so that they could study with Aisling. The school granted their request, and every day the three of them studied at the library together. Aisling said she could not have done it without their support.

Esther and I went for a lot of walks and visited Rainbow Haven Beach a couple of times. The following Wednesday, as we drove to the airport, she said she was happy that I was doing so well; after she got home she called me every day for over a year.

On Monday of the following week, a large cardboard box with Deirdre's belongings arrived. Although I had thrown out everything that she had in the hospital, Aisling and I felt comfortable enough going through the box. Aisling found a ring that Deirdre's cousins Natalie and Jason had given her for her twenty-first birthday—Deirdre was working in Ireland for the summer at that time. The ring had a design of a mythical Irish character and Deirdre wore it constantly before her finger size shrunk during her illness.

Natalie and Jason seldom called; and yet, Natalie called fifteen minutes before Aisling found the ring, and Jason called fifteen minutes after. They loved to tell the story about Deirdre and the ring. On her birthday night, a group of them had gone out to a restaurant. After they gave the ring to Deirdre, she kept repeating how much she loved it, pushing it forward on her finger so that it flew across the restaurant floor a number of times.

After we went through her belongings, Aisling took most of Deirdre's clothes and we gave some to Deirdre's friends. The second box arrived by mail two weeks later. I went to pick it up at the post office but returned home empty-handed. I had to return with Deirdre's cremation certificate before they would release it.

After Esther left, I was a little nervous about being in the house by myself, but I continued to sleep normally. At night before I went to sleep I would look out the window and, in my thoughts, tell Deirdre that I knew she was out there somewhere among the stars that were sprinkled across the dark sky. Before closing my eyes I would thank my spirit and the universe for helping me through this time. I awoke every morning around 8:00.

At first I was puzzled as to why I was doing so well. I'd felt worse after much smaller losses than this one. Whenever a feeling of deep sadness came over me, in less than ten seconds I would think of Deirdre, and an all-encompassing feeling of profound love would flow through me, pushing away the sadness. I began to realize that it was indeed *her*, in her spirit form, lifting me up, preventing me from falling into an abyss of depression.

People had given me high-quality self-help books on grieving, but I had read similar ones over the years. Three weeks after Deirdre passed over I was at a second-hand bookshop with my friend Barbara. As I was rummaging through a pile of books in a bin, I picked up one called *Talking to Heaven* by James Van Praagh. I'd never heard of the book or the author before. I read on the back cover that James Van Praagh was a medium; I decided this book might be interesting, and bought it.

When I went home and after I browsed through different chapters, I realized it was the perfect book for me right now.

Van Praagh's book reinforced my belief that Deirdre was still around; I know that finding this book wasn't mere coincidence. He wrote that people's personalities don't change when they pass over. Deirdre's hasn't; she's still as persuasive as ever.

Later I was given a book called *Journey of the Soul*, written by British writer Brenda Davies, a former surgeon—now a psychiatrist and a medium. In her book she writes about spirituality and the relationship it has to emotional and physical well-being.

Deirdre made great efforts to connect with me, especially in the first year after her passing.

On a warm afternoon, two weeks after she passed over, I was painting my back deck, hoping to get some mental therapy. As I pushed the paintbrush up over a rail, a monarch butterfly landed in front of my brush, and despite my rush to get the painting done, it immediately made me stop to look at its beautiful orange and black colours. It stayed a few seconds longer than was usual for a butterfly. Thoughts of Deirdre rushed to me right away and I had a gut feeling that the experience had something to do with her.

During the next year, on four different occasions overhead lights flickered, making me think of Deirdre, and later I realized that she was cautioning me about something. She doesn't do it anymore. In the book *Talking to Heaven*, I read that spirits may try to communicate in the first year or so after they've passed over.

In September of that year, on a beautiful Sunday morning, I decided to visit Rainbow Haven Beach. I thought about asking one of my friends along, but then decided to go alone. As I sat and read, enjoying the quietness of the beach – not thinking about Deirdre—a seagull appeared at the water's edge in front of me. For about ten minutes, it sat there looking straight at me.

Thoughts of Deirdre filled my mind and I felt a beautiful sense of peace that intensified over the ten minutes. As the seagull flew away to the left of me, it swooped down to the spot where we had scattered Deirdre's ashes, barely touching the water before lifting back up again and flying off towards the horizon.

I headed home and glanced around for something to read.

Without thinking, I picked up a book that sat on the coffee table. It was called *Angels of the Maritimes* by Karen Forrest. A few days before, my friend Evelyn Edgett had loaned it to me. I absently opened it to a page and my eyes locked on this paragraph.

> **Our deceased loved ones often find creative ways to send us a message reassuring us that they are well and at peace. One common sign from a deceased loved one is through butterflies and birds (and other animals). The butterfly or bird will stand out because it will fly closer to you than normal and act out of character, for example sitting still longer or looking at you directly. Also, as you admire the butterfly or bird, you will suddenly be reminded of your deceased loved one and feel a sensation of peace overflow your body.**

I was amazed to read this after the experience I had had. I assumed Deirdre was letting me know how happy she was; she can't be too far from heaven.

The intuitive mind is a sacred gift and the rational mind is a faithful servant. We have created a society that honours the servant and has forgotten the gift. —Albert Einstein

Chapter 24

UNCONVENTIONAL COUNSELLING

Life is thickly sown with thorns, and I know no other remedy than to pass quickly through them. The longer we dwell on our misfortunes, the greater is their power to harm us. —Voltaire

In early July, I did a three-week nursing assignment in a small community in Nunavut. I had worked there for six weeks during February and March of that year. I wanted to get away and clear my mind, but wasn't ready for a holiday that could provide too much time to think. Throughout the three weeks, I felt the same as I had during my previous visits there; I enjoyed the intensity of the work, the tranquil walks out in the tundra, and the authenticity and wholesomeness of the Inuit.

Aisling and Conor went about their lives as they normally did. Conor, who says little about his emotions, seemed reasonably happy anytime we met. In August, the three of us went to see a play by Thornton Wilder, *Our Town*—part of an outdoor theatre.

Deirdre's friends Katie, Ben, Susan, and Alex were the main actors. In one scene the spirits of people who used to live in the town sat on chairs in a field and talked to one another. Katie, the main character in the scene, wearing a long white cotton dress, played the part of a twenty-six-year-old-woman who had just died after childbirth.

As part of her school's schedule that year, Aisling had two months off. She went to Ireland and Spain for three weeks with two of her friends, Katie and Ellen. Our relatives in different parts of Ireland, delighted to see Aisling, showed them great hospitality.

On July 14, the night before Deirdre's birthday, I was in Nunavut. When I turned on the TV that evening, it showed a documentary on Mount Koyasan,

Japan. A year before, around that same week, Deirdre, Aisling, Conor and I had spent a wonderful two days in Mount Koyasan. We were intrigued by the quaintness of the temple where we stayed—one of over one hundred in the small town—and the huge cemetery, with numerous gigantic cypress trees, where one thousand monks were buried. To get there we had taken a train and cable car up through the wooded mountains.

When I saw the documentary I felt it was Deirdre's gift to me, bringing me happy memories on her birthday.

On July 15, Deirdre's birthday, I called Aisling in Ireland. She was staying at my brother Doney's farm. It sits on a hill overlooking the Shannon Estuary, and above a little village called Foynes in County Limerick—where I grew up. Aisling and Deirdre had spent a lot of summers there, enjoying the freedom of playing in the fields and hay barns with their cousins John, Karen, and Sarah.

Aisling and her friends had planned to stay two nights, but they left the next morning; too many memories. She and I vowed that in the future, we would be together on Deirdre's birthday.

I made a chocolate birthday cake and shared it with the staff in the Health Centre in Nunavut.

Over the course of that summer I had some sad days, but nothing unbearable. I kept myself busy doing different projects around the house and garden.

Daichi and I phoned one another frequently. He was very sad and lonely. He said he talked to his mother every day.

Aisling did well all summer. She went back to class and began her clerkship that September. During the second week, as part of an exam, she interviewed a simulated patient—a person hired and trained to act as a patient. For the interview she had to show how she would go about informing a patient that they had terminal cancer. Later she said, "It was excruciating."

The reality of Deirdre's passing suddenly hit her, replacing the denial stage like a broken blister. I was still in Nunavut at the time.

It was painful for Aisling to talk about Deirdre and her own loss. She had to force her attention outward, to focus intensely on her studies to get through medical school.

She experienced another blow the following January when she did a surgical rotation at the VG hospital. The surgical offices where she reported were just off the corridor between 8A and 8B. She would often see Nebojsa and the nurses who had looked after Deirdre, and even though she managed to avoid them, camouflaged by blue operating room (OR) scrubs and hat, she later said that she felt "awful" when she saw them.

In November of that year, Aisling moved back home. Even though we were both away a lot, and at different times, it was comforting to have one another's presence in the house.

Aisling did electives in different places—across Canada, Ireland, and Tanzania—and I did assignments in Nunavut. Living together was a positive move for both of us.

She has since moved out, and starts a pediatric residency program in July of this year. We still speak to one another often and remain very close. Conor is also moving ahead with his life, independent, trying to figure out his future career.

One morning in late November of 2008, after I got up, I had a sudden impulse to call Deborah Young, a psychic astrologer. I had been to see her two years before but hadn't thought about going to her since then. I think of *reputable* psychic astrologers not as "fortune tellers" but as innate counsellors. I looked for Deborah's number in the phone book and found it right away. I left a message. She returned my call that afternoon.

I told her about Deirdre and asked her for an appointment. She had a year's waiting list, but because of the circumstances she agreed to see me in January. After I gave her my birth date and Deirdre's, she matter-of-factly said, "It's good that you're coming in January. Your July daughter wants to communicate some things to you." I believe that Deirdre persuaded me to call Deborah.

Over time I became familiar with Deirdre's tactics of putting ideas in my head—all had very positive outcomes that came from her altruistic love.

In early January it was blowing snow as I set off from my house on the fifteen-minute walk to Deborah's office. I was excited and looking forward to hearing Deirdre's messages.

When I arrived, Deborah was surprised I had made it there. She showed me into a room that was small and cosy, with Tibetan carvings and other icons decorating the space. I sat on a couch that was out a little from the wall, and Deborah sat on a chair diagonal to me. She had long blond hair and wore a stylish blue dress.

As a preamble we talked about the weather.

Then she began by telling me that I was born with an energy that gave me the ability to cope and navigate through something like Deirdre's passing in a very amazing way, and she also told me that I knew that Deirdre wasn't really gone. She said that I listen to my spirit, knowing it to be right—and that I let it guide me. I was walking two paths. One path was very uplifting, yet on the other path I was trying to sort out and rid myself of painful things.

Not knowing or having met Deirdre, she went on to say that Deirdre was "funny as hell, she could have been a comedian," and she said that Deirdre had had a penicillin allergy. She had been cremated. She scuba dived and she danced. Deborah explained that Deirdre was letting her know these things to assure me of her presence. She spoke of Deirdre's "spunky charm," how she championed the underdog, and that she had solid friends. She said Deirdre was very kind and saw me as her rock and knew that I would always be there for her.

When I asked about the butterfly and the seagull, she said that winged creatures can act as messengers from the spirit world. The monarch butterfly communicated that Deirdre had been beautifully transformed, the seagull signified looking beyond what we see with the naked eye, and that Deirdre was close by in another form.

"You haven't got rid of her clothes yet," she said. When I told her no, she said that Deirdre wanted them to go to a women's shelter. I took a few bags of her clothes to a shelter the next week. Deborah asked if "Lord of the Dance" was played at her funeral. When I answered yes, she said, "Deirdre loved that." She said that we planned her funeral exactly as Deirdre wanted it. Deirdre wants us to have fun on her birthdays.

When I asked about the short relationship with Daichi, Deborah said that it was wonderful that he gave her the gift of a healthy romantic love before she passed over. Deirdre still loved him, but in time she would get over that and help him find a good partner. She helps her family and friends, spends time with Esther—

Esther kept telling me that Deirdre was on her mind all the time.

She said Deirdre knows what's best for us now and tries to steer us in that direction. She said that Deirdre was outside a lot.

I told her I was a little concerned that Deirdre didn't know about her passing beforehand.

"Oh, she was totally prepared for it in spirit," she said confidently. "It was a very smooth transition." She agreed that Deirdre's soul had left her body before she stopped breathing and that she had been trying to comfort us.

Before we said our good-byes, she gave me other advice about my everyday life—some of it coming from Deirdre.

Even though I was emotionally drained, I was excited to have my feelings validated about Deirdre's presence.

Because I've had numerous life changes, I had seen three different psychic astrologers over a twenty-year period. I would go once a year for my "psychic counselling." Because their higher-than-average intuitiveness gave them the ability to recognize what was inside my mind, they gave me advice and hope that has been encouraging over the years. I was given just enough information; it wouldn't influence the choices that I alone had to make, and be accountable for, in my journey in life. They've never scared me or told me anything outlandish—like I'd win the lottery.

On earlier occasions I had been given hints about losing a child such as, "Did you have a miscarriage or lose a child?" and "Someone very close to you will need a lot of help in the hospital." I never thought much about it until after Deirdre passed over. I realize that Deirdre's path was already destined and that I couldn't control it.

This awareness prevented me from experiencing guilt, anger, resentfulness, or jealousy—emotions that can be crippling. Instead, I only had sadness to deal with, which was negated by Deirdre's pure love, and the love of the universe, of God.

In September of 2009, while I was out for a walk, I decided to drop into a store that sold books and other resource material on spirituality. A notice on their bulletin board advertised psychic readings by a lady named Kelliena. I looked at the notice, asked the shop owner about Kelliena, and before I knew it I was planted on a chair in front of a young lady for my fifteen-minute reading.

She asked if I had any questions and I said no, I didn't. Then she enquired if someone close to me had passed over within the past two years. When I answered yes, she pointed to the air beside her and said, "She's standing right here. I saw her come in with you." She said that Deirdre wanted me to look in her hard-covered diary. She told me there was a bookmark inside that had ribbons on it, and I would get some inspiration for my writing there.

She asked that I look at some of Deirdre's books, and Deirdre would guide me to one that she wanted me to read. Deirdre wants me to look for a lock of her hair, which I saved when she was a newborn baby; it would be in her baby book. I didn't think I had saved any and told Kelliena that—Deirdre was born with a full head of hair. Like Deborah, she said that Deirdre was outside a lot and that she helps us, she's very happy, and she tries to make me laugh more.

After I went home, I looked in Deirdre's baby book and there in a little paper pocket was a lock of her dark newborn hair. I could feel her love when I touched it.

I found the hard-covered diary with a bookmark in it. The bookmark, belonging to Aisling, was made of wood and had ribbons carved in it. I read the diary and was even more inspired to write. I have recorded some of Deirdre's words at the beginning of some chapters of this book.

Deirdre acquired mononucleosis (mono), a viral illness caused by the Epstein-Barr virus, during her first year in university. Apart from swollen glands and some discomfort, she recovered in less than a week. Even though mono symptoms are often minor, on rare occasions, as in Deirdre's case, the Epstein-Barr virus can weaken the immune system significantly. I used to think that Deirdre's eczema rash, which began after she'd had the virus, was a result of her weakened immune system. Since she passed over, I've wondered if the leukemia was another consequence of this.

After I visited Kelliena, I rooted around in the basement of my house and found a book of Deirdre's by Douglas Coupland called *Girlfriend in a Coma*. I opened it and read the first few pages.

The first two paragraphs were about a high school student named Jared who had died. One day while he was playing football, he blacked out. He thought he was just having a severe relapse of mono from two years earlier. A few hours later, after he woke up, he was diagnosed with leukemia and died three months later. In the next paragraph a sentence read, "My life was happy and full and short; Earth was kind to me and my bout with cancer was my Great Experience."

Was Deirdre trying to tell me something?

I'm thankful for the way events happened. It was a blessing that we didn't know about Deirdre's dismal prospects of survival and that we never lost hope for the entirety of her illness. When Dr. White said "I'm sorry" that morning in her room, I realize now what he alluded to. To keep both types of leukemia in remission was a major medical challenge.

Later, after Deirdre passed over, I read an article that said only about 7 percent of people who acquire acute leukemia get "biphenotypic leukemia." This is the combination of both types, myeloid and lymphoblastic.

Deirdre and Aisling having supper at the temple in Mount Koyasan

Chapter 25
OUR GUIDE

I believe that imagination is stronger than knowledge—myth
is more potent than history—dreams are more powerful
than facts—hope always triumphs over experience—laughter
is the cure for grief—love is stronger than death.
—Robert Fulghum

In March of 2010, I visited Deborah Young again. She talked about this book.

"Deirdre is absolutely thrilled that you're writing about her. She pushes you and she is right there with you when you do write." Until then, I had wondered why I sit on the green couch for over eight hours every day, my laptop on my knee, feeling I have to get this book written as soon as possible.

I went to Italy in May of 2009, and during the two days I spent in Rome, I thought about Deirdre most of the time. I supposed the reason she was on my mind so much was because I knew how much she appreciated art. Deborah asked me if I thought about Deirdre a lot while I was in Italy. She told me that Deirdre "hitched a ride" there with me and hung around for a while. She asked if I had bought a red purse from a seller on the sidewalk and when I told her I had, she said, "Deirdre was with you and she picked it out. It wasn't her style but she knew it was yours."

Ben sent me an e-mail in April of this year. He wrote about his chats with Deirdre in the hospital and how much he enjoyed them. He observed how she retained "her beauty, her glow" throughout her illness—despite the unattractive hospital gowns. He realized it was her spirit that made her look beautiful.

He recalled that when she talked to him on the phone the day that she passed over, she said, "You gave me a stroke" in the same playful tone that she used to yell, "*Sarry!*" when she sent his player back home in the board game.

Ben said he will never forget Deirdre and he recognizes her, at unexpected moments, in the beauty around him.

Aisling's graduation gala was on May 29, 2010. The dancing went on until after 1:30 AM on May 30—the same date and time that Deirdre passed over two years before.

One of the pages in the gala program pamphlet named twenty-five people who had all passed on. Deirdre's name was among them. A notation above the names on the page was apt:

"Throughout our lifetime there have been many inspiring stories and individuals who have shaped our reasons and desire to pursue the study of medicine. Despite their passing, the following individuals continue to guide us through this remarkable and privileged journey."

Perfect timing for Deirdre's anniversary.

The next day, May 30, 2010, was the second anniversary of Deirdre's passing. I was sitting out on my back deck—the same deck where the butterfly had landed while I was painting shortly after Deirdre passed on. This time, a monarch butterfly landed on the floor of the deck close by me and spread its wings. It stayed there for about five minutes. I sensed that this was a message from Deirdre, arriving as it did on her anniversary.

Two years have passed since Deirdre has changed form. When people tell me how amazed they are at how well I am doing, I just tell them that's because she's still here and that, no, I'm not having a psychotic episode.

Every day as I grew up, my mother reminded me about our soul that never dies. Deirdre has proven that what my mother told me is true. I'm thankful that Deirdre guided me to Deborah and Kelliena, choosing them as her emissaries. Both have said that she is thankful that I am aware of her continued existence and that I communicate and listen to her. It makes me sad to think how upset she'd be if I ignored her. But, if I didn't listen, I know that with her courage, her originality, and most of all, her wisdom, she'd find some creative way to make her presence known to me.

We still communicate with Daichi. He says he feels that Deirdre helps him every day, and he thanks God for allowing him to meet her. He sent me an e-mail in May of this year, telling me that he was preparing for entrance exams to law school. He was offered a big promotion by the company he works for, but declined. Instead, he gave his notice of resignation for July, allowing himself time to study. He wrote that if he hadn't met Deirdre he would have taken the promotion; she had taught him to pursue his dreams.

As Deirdre's family and friends, and those of us who ask for her help, move forward on our journeys in life, I know that for now, Deirdre gives us the occasional loving push in the right direction.

I'm sure that in her present form, she continues to balance work and play, while she also helps our world, carrying messages like a mercurial butterfly; burning the candle at both ends.

Knowing that Deirdre's spirit is out there, moving gracefully between the earth and the stars, enjoying measureless freedom as she travels at such great heights—open to new things, places, and experiences—makes me feel happy and privileged that she chose me as her mother.